THE INTERNATIONAL JOURNAL OF ETHICAL LEADERSHIP

Volume 9
Summer 2022

The International Journal of Ethical Leadership
Case Western Reserve University
Editor-in-Chief: Shannon E. French, Inamori Professor in Ethics and Director, Inamori International Center for Ethics and Excellence
Executive Editor: Michael Scharf, Dean of the School of Law, John Deaver Drinko-Baker & Hostetler Professor of Law, and Director, Frederick K. Cox International Law Center
Senior Executive Editor: Beth Trecasa, Acting Director, Inamori International Center for Ethics and Excellence
Copyeditor: Thea Ledendecker

The International Journal of Ethical Leadership, Volume 9, Summer 2022

ISSN 2326-7461
ISBN: 978-1-62922-247-9

For additional information, please contact inamoricenter@case.edu
or visit case.edu/inamori

Contents

Letters

Inamori Ethics Prize Recipients

Articles

Transcripts

Message from the Editor

Beth Trecasa
Acting Director,
Inamori International Center for Ethics and Excellence,
Case Western Reserve University

Individual Ethical Leadership, Responsible Global Citizenship

In this shared world where pandemic pressures persist, historic challenges remain, and new battles begin, there is a tension between returning to life at another time and adapting to current realities. We pull each other in opposing directions because despite our differences and distances, we are still connected, locally and globally.

The past two years have made our interconnectedness particularly, and sometimes painfully, clear. At our best, human connection and collective action create not only positive change, but unfathomable progress, solutions, and even cures. However, in far too many ways, these same tools cause catastrophic regression. At our worst, we incite violence and enact unjust wars. We continue methods and systems of oppression and call them traditions.

Many turn to local and global leadership for direction, for resources, and for refuge. They should. And thankfully, some will be able to answer that call. When other leaders, or worse systems of justice and safety, falter or fail, it is the everyday efforts of ethical people that not only keep us all moving forward, but also restore hope in a way that only humanity can.

Showing and receiving empathy. Seeing the inherent worth and dignity in every person and being seen. Doing the most responsible thing possible and experiencing the benefit of someone else's good choice. Thoughtful efforts and intentional actions. Everyday ethics can also be contagious. We are inspired by neighbors helping neighbors, strangers supporting strangers. We are better when we consider the well-being of not only those we know, but also those we will never meet. We are better when we think globally and act locally. Because ultimately, for better or worse, we are all co-inhabitants of the same shared world.

While systems of injustice endure, or just crumble slowly, everyday efforts of ethical people remind us that justice and equity are still possible, even if not always immediate. Individual ethical leadership grows into positive collective action, into social justice, and eventually systemic change. At our best, we pull each other up and forward because despite our differences and distances, we are still connected, locally and globally.

For the past ten years, *The International Journal of Ethical Leadership* has strived to contribute to the interdisciplinary, international conversation on what ethical leadership requires, but also what ethical leadership can do. Ethics requires genuine efforts toward justice and equity because this gives every person their best chance to flourish. Ethics gives our shared world a chance to flourish.

In this ninth volume, our contributors and contributions come to us from Africa, Argentina, Australia, Turkey, and the United States and collectively cover a range of perspectives from emerging students to esteemed faculty and distinguished practitioners. This volume is dedicated to our authors; my trusted advisors; and ethical people who contribute to positive human progress every day by striving to make good choices for themselves and for their local and global neighbors. Frankly, I'm rooting for us all.

A Path to Global Justice
My Insider's View

Silvia Fernández de Gurmendi
2020 Inamori Ethics Prize Recipient

Thank you very much. Actually, it was good to hide behind my mask. Now, I can see that I am—really this is a very emotional moment for me, thank you, thank you very much, and let me start by saying good evening to all of you, and I would like to start by expressing my deep, deep, gratitude to Provost Ben Vinson, Professor Shannon French, Case Western Reserve University leadership, the Inamori Foundation, the Inamori International Center for Ethics and Excellence, and the donors and community partners. I'm honored and humbled by the Inamori Ethics Prize that has been awarded to me. I'm also a bit intimidated, I have to say, by the list of extraordinary men and women that have preceded me. I am not extraordinary by any means, but I hope that at least I share some of their commitment and enthusiasm for a good cause, as well as the conviction that by working hard with others toward a well-defined goal, we can contribute in concrete ways to a better, more ethical world.

These contributions can take many forms and relate to achievements in most diverse areas, such as genetics, business, the environment, philosophy, policy, the arts, or, as in my case, justice, or, more specifically, international criminal justice. Justice, in general, and international criminal justice in particular, are closely related to ethics. Indeed, ethics are the very foundation of the criminal justice system. Ethics help us as a society to define what we consider to be reprehensible conduct, what an acceptable punishment, and what an acceptable manner to determine that such a contact may be attributed to an individual in a concrete case. A national system of justice is indeed based on standards and values generally shared by the society to which it belongs and from which it derives, but what about an international system of justice? What would the values and standards be for such a system, and who needs to share them? At the international level, we often speak about the international community, but it suffices to look around into our fragmented, divided world to realize that the notion refers at best to a broad and ill-defined group of people and governments of the world with various and often-opposed standards. Are any of these standards or values shared by all, or at least a large majority of the members of such group? If yes, how do we then identify them, give them a concrete form, and apply them in practice?

These were some of the questions we had to ask ourselves when we embarked in the creation and setup of the International Criminal Court to fight impunity for atrocity crimes at the global level. We had to find the way of aligning this loosely conformed international community with a common vision. We did it through a multilateral process open to all, but led by some. I have been part of this process that is still ongoing since its inception until now in various capacities including as negotiator, judge, president of the court, and now as president of the Assembly of States Parties. I would like to use this opportunity to share with you my insider's view on the path we followed which could serve, I think, as a model for initiatives in other domains as well. I will focus on how we succeeded in bringing together this otherwise fragmented international community to pursue the global goal of creating an international criminal court. How we managed to identify together the values, the standards, and procedures on which to base it and make it operational. And finally, I will share with you what we are doing today at this very moment to keep it alive and relevant. This is a long story, but I will focus on three main central acts of this thirty-year-long story.

The first act was about gathering support for the creation of the court and defining the common standards. In the days that followed the creation of the International Criminal Court, many grand phrases were set and written. The famous phrase by the French writer Victor Hugo was often repeated. The phrase goes, "Nothing is as powerful as an idea whose time has come." A good phrase for sure, but it doesn't fully convey the difficult, hazardous process involved in materializing an idea. As history well demonstrates, good ideas do not flourish by themselves. On the contrary, they need to be identified as such and be promoted with vision, perseverance, and hard work. The International Criminal Court (the ICC), was created in Rome on the 17th of July, 1998, after some four years of intense negotiations that took place at the UN headquarters in New York. Only hours before the dramatic adoption of the founding treaty of the Rome Statute, many continued to think that an agreement was not possible, that the time for such an ambitious institution had simply not come. And yet four years before, at the time of my arrival in New York as a young diplomat, the idea that international justice for the gravest international crimes was crucial for sustainable peace was gaining momentum at the United Nations.

The end of the Cold War had altered, dramatically, the relations between big powers, which in turn had had a huge impact on the work of the Security Council and of the United Nations more broadly. A few months before I arrived, the Security Council had reached an unprecedented agreement to create an ad hoc international criminal tribunal to deal with genocide, crimes against humanity, and war crimes in forming Yugoslavia. A similar tribunal would follow in 1994 to address the genocide committed in Rwanda. The same year, the International Law Commission (the ILC) submitted to the General Assembly at the UN a draft statute for an international criminal court to deal with the same type of crimes on a permanent basis, wherever committed. Most importantly, the ILC also recommended states to convene immediately a diplomatic conference to negotiate the creation of such a court on the basis of its draft. The draft and the recommendations were received with great enthusiasm by many. However, despite the growing acceptance for international justice, the proposal to convene a diplomatic conference immediately to create an independent global court was a bridge too far for a significant minority of states, which included the United States and all other permanent members of the Security Council. As we all know, if you want to kill a good idea, you create a committee to deal with it, so instead of immediately convening a diplomatic conference, not one but two committees were successively put in place at which the ILC draft was considered during the four years that followed. However, protracted discussions that took place at both committees did not kill the idea. Enthusiasm survived and actually grew thanks to an intense campaign by states and civil society organizations to promote the court and its expeditious establishment.

To this effect, NGOs created the coalition for the establishment of the International Criminal Court. States founded the Like-Minded group. I was co-founder of the latter, which comprised only a handful of state representatives at the beginning. We used to meet in small side rooms of the UN. In one of our missions, we were very vocal about our existence and goals but remained deliberately vague about our actual composition because we wanted to give the impression that we were numerous, powerful, unstoppable, and indeed we were. The group grew quickly, to the point that we stopped counting and became more demanding. We ceased to focus solely on accelerating the creation of the court and started to develop the principles that we considered essential for an independent, strong, and impartial institution. States that wanted to become a member of the Like-Minded group were now required to adhere to these principles.

By the time of the conference, we were a big and powerful group of more than sixty states of all regions. We had been careful to avoid the north-south divide and had managed to engage states of all continents to ensure a cross-regional approach to the matter. The NGO coalition had also grown quantitatively and qualitatively. By the time of the conference, it comprised hundreds of organizations that promoted the court, put forward policy and technical documents, and gave assistance to smaller delegations. The like-minded group working in partnership with the NGO coalition was an extremely powerful voice. It provided initiatives, strategies, and support to the leadership of the conference. I was myself part of both, as vice president of the negotiating body of the conference, as well as a member of the core group of states that steered the like-minded. The four previous years of preparative discussions had been extremely useful to address multiple political, substantive, and procedural matters; however, most issues remained unresolved by the time the conference started. At the conference, finding common ground among hundreds of participants from all regions required extensive and complex negotiations. We consider that the recourse to a vote as a way of solving disputes among delegations was not an option. We were convinced that such a global institution could not be built on occasional majorities, but through very large agreements on shared standards. But did we have any meaningful common standards at all? The fact that we had managed to convene the conference to create the court was a positive sign already, but what type of court based on what values: Western values, African values, Asian, Latin American?

In order to narrow the differences, we also narrow the scope of our discussions to a very limited number of the most serious international crimes. Genocide, war crimes, crimes against humanity, and also aggression, which found its way into the statue despite the controversies. But even with relation to these core crimes, agreements were difficult, because only then genocide had a broadly accepted definition. For this first time ever, we embarked in a multilateral effort to achieve a detailed and comprehensive definition of war crimes and crimes against humanity. The definitions were supposed to be only a codification of pre-existing norms, but ended up including some ambitious, innovative, and progressive elements. Most notably, the war crimes and crimes against humanity incorporated new sexual offenses and a gender perspective. Furthermore, the definition of war crimes did not abolish, but significantly blurred the traditional distinction between international and non-international armed conflicts. The definition of aggression would come later in 2010 at the review conference held in Kampala, Uganda.

In addition to the crimes, and many other crucial institutional features, we also needed to determine the criminal procedures—namely, how someone would be investigated, arrested, transferred, tried, and eventually punished by the court. Last but not least, we needed to determine the appropriate system for victims' participation and reparations, something that was at the time totally unprecedented in international criminal justice. The principles inscribed in the International Covenant on Civil and Political Rights, such as the presumption of innocence and the right to an adequate defense, represented standards widely recognized by the world, and constituted therefore a very good starting point, and indeed all these fundamental principles are now inscribed in the Rome Statute. But, in addition to general principles, some insisted that it was the prerogative of states to prescribe in great detail how the entire criminal process would unfold, and what would be the appropriate penalty. While all other international courts and tribunals had been allowed to adopt their own rules for the conduct of the proceedings, the International Criminal Court was to apply state-made law only. The legislative effort by states required a constant comparative effort among various legal systems of the world. A global court could not favor one system in detriment of others. Indeed, it had to represent all and attach to none. Again, states embarked in a lengthy process of negotiations to agree on a workable procedural scheme.

Judge James Crawford, who chaired the work for the International Criminal Court and the International Law Commission, once described how they have "to contend with the tendency of each duly socialized lawyer to prefer his own criminal justice system's values and institutions." And I can fully corroborate this tendency, as I was personally in charge of leading this international drafting of the criminal procedures for many years—before, during, and after the Rome Conference. There was a permanent clash, and endless discussions between representatives of the two major criminal law systems of the world: the common law and the civil law system, based on arguments of efficiency and firmness, and also a certain degree of cultural chauvinism. At the start of the conference there were still hundreds of points of controversy with numerous options of suboptions that had to be addressed and solved, and they were solved, one by one, in marathon accessions of the conference.

The result was the elaboration of an innovative, unique, hybrid system which combines elements of the common law and the civil law systems. The product of the extensive negotiations of substantive law and procedure is now contained in the Rome Statute and its complementary instruments adopted two years after the conference. They reflect common standards achieved by consensus across regions, in discussion open to all states of the world, including all major powers. Among them, the United States supported the creation of the court and participated actively in the negotiation, contributing greatly to all aspects of this framework with a large and capable delegation. While all these standards were agreed by consensus, the Rome Statute was itself put to a vote at the end of the conference at the request of the American delegation. The breaking point was related to the exercise of jurisdiction by the court over nationals of a non-state party. Seven countries voted against; 21 abstained; 120 voted in favor.

The adoption was accompanied by an explosion of applause, emotion, and tears. In light of this final vote, some wondered whether there would be sufficient support to ratify the treaty and set up the institution. Like four years before, some considered, again, that the time had not come. For them, the court would not see the light, at least not in our lifetimes. And yet, the second act to which I now turn had already begun. Act two was about gathering support for the setup of the court. Immediately after Rome, the NGO Coalition of the Like-Minded reassembled forces and engaged in an active campaign to obtain the large number of sixty ratifications required. Exceeding all expectations, this was achieved in less than four years. The treaty entered into force on the first of July, 2002, and the first Assembly of State Parties was convened.

The assembly envisaged in the statute is the oversight of the legislative body of the court. It is composed of representatives of all the states that have ratified or acceded to the Rome Statute, currently 123. As its first session, the assembly adopted all the instruments complementary to the Rome Statute, including the rules of procedure and evidence, and took all necessary decisions to set up the court. Months later, it elected the first eighteen judges and the prosecutor, who were sworn in in the semester of 2003. Soon afterwards, investigations started, and proceedings began. The first suspects started to arrive in The Hague. They were tried; some of them were convicted. The first trial of the court was against Thomas Lubanga, a Congolese rebel leader accused of forcefully recruiting and enlisting child soldiers. As part of the final allegations at this historic first trial, Ben Ferencz, former prosecutor at Nuremberg, appeared before the judges to contribute to the pleadings of the prosecution. The International Criminal Court was finally operational and demonstrating it could deliver justice, against all odds.

The first investigations and trial were followed by others, and gradually the court became the large institution that it is today, with its headquarters at The Hague in the Netherlands, a liaison office in New York, and seven field offices in various countries in Africa and in Georgia, Asia. As of today, the prosecutor has opened fourteen investigations, most of them in Africa, and three in Asia: Afghanistan, Georgia, and Myanmar. The court has issued ten convictions, four acquittals, and thirteen people wanted by the court are currently at large.

Despite all this movement and growth, the enthusiasm of the negotiating years gradually turned into disappointment. The court was accused of focusing too much on Africa, of not having enough cases, of being too expensive, too inefficient. There were threats of massive withdrawals and two states, Burundi and the Philippines, actually withdrew in 2017 and 2018. There were politically motivated attacks against the court, but also good-faith criticism from strong supporters. By the time I joined the court as a judge in 2010, internal and external problems were already mounting. Proceedings were slow and convoluted, and interactions between the various organs of the court—the presidency, the judiciary, the prosecutor, and the registry—and within each organ, were difficult. Despite constant appeals by the Assembly of State Parties to pursue a one-court principle, fragmentation prevailed.

The lack of cohesion was evident within the judiciary itself. Judges coming from all regions of the world had, like negotiators before them, the tendency to favor their respective legal system, and tended to interpret and apply the ICC legal framework through the lens of their own. Furthermore, as judges sit in separate chambers, the same matter result in one chamber could very well lead to a similar discussion but different solution in another one. This did not contribute to forge a stable, consistent, and predictable jurisprudence. The replacement of a third of all judges every three years did not make cohesion any easier. I was struck by a sense of déjà vu when I had my first discussions in chambers with my fellow judges. I felt I had ventured in a time tunnel and taken a trip back to the negotiations and procedures that were held fifteen years ago. The ICC community was encountering similar problems to those confronted by the international community before, and that risked undermining the common standards forged in Rome.

External and internal observers worried, and initiatives to improve started to emerge and be developed by various organs of the court, including some concrete amendments proposals to the legal framework. From 2012 onwards, efforts to take stock of lessons learned and improve the work accelerated under the supervision of the Assembly of the Parties. Upon my election as president of the court in 2015, I made it a top priority of my three-year presidency to enhance the overall management of the court and the efficiency and effectiveness of judicial proceedings. I emphasized the importance of cohesion and collegiality. To increase cohesion of the court, I applied some of the techniques that had succeeded to bring some unity within the international community in the years of negotiations. At the court, I strived to improve decision-making on joint strategies and policy issues by strengthening or creating inter-organ platforms for dialogue. Within the judiciary, I tried to replace fragmentation by collective thinking. For the first time, all judges engaged in a joint assessment of methods of work, the legal framework, and their practices for each phase of the proceedings. They did this through annual judges retreats, regular judges meeting organized within each judicial division, and the appointment of individual judges as focal points to lead discussions on specific issues. Gradually, all judges, as well as members of the legal support staff, became involved in various ways in the review of proceedings with a view to agreeing on the best practices to streamline proceedings and, if needed, propose discrete amendments to the applicable rules.

By the time I left in March 2018, we had achieved some positive and tangible results at the court in general, and at the court room specifically, including a noticeable reduction of the length of trial proceedings. However, it was clear that much more needed to be done to achieve drastic systemic changes. Not only did this not happen, but on the contrary, some institutional and judicial setbacks triggered, again, serious concerns. By then, patience had run out.

In June 2019, four former presidents of the Assembly of the Parties reflected the general sentiment in a public letter entitled "The Court Needs Fixing." In the letter, they noted that, I quote, "The powerful impact of the court's central message is too often not matched by its performance as a judicial institution. We are disappointed by the quality of some of the judicial proceedings, frustrated by some of the results, and exasperated by the management deficiencies that prevent the court from living up to its full potential." According to them, it was time to make a new deal between the ICC and the state parties. In the spirit that made them succeed in Rome, importantly, they acknowledge that this new deal required not only the efforts of the court to improve its own performance, but also implied at the other end an obligation of states to, and I quote, "fully embrace the potential of the ICC as a central institution in the fight against impunity." States, they said, have to stand up for the ICC mission to be judicially independent, even, or in particular, in situations where that may be politically inconvenient. And states need to give the court the resources it needs to do the job.

As a first step toward this new deal, they suggested to undertake an independent assessment of the court's functioning to provide court officials and non-state holders with a common point of reference going forward. In the same year the recommendation was accepted at the Assembly of the State Parties, and the assembly launched a process of review of the entire Rome Statute system. This is the process that is currently unfolding in what is the third and last act in my presentation to you. This third act is about gathering support for the review of the Rome Statute system. Indeed, following this eloquent letter at the end of 2019, the Assembly of State Parties established an independent expert review with the overall mandate to make concrete, achievable, and actionable recommendations aimed at enhancing the performance, efficiency, and effectiveness of the court and the Rome Statute system as a whole. To this effect, nine experts were appointed from various regions of the world, who presented by the end of 2020 a detailed report elaborated on the basis of hundreds of written submissions, interviews, and meetings with all relevant stakeholders, including ICC former and current elected officers and staff members, legal representatives of victims and accused persons, NGOs, and academia.

The voluminous report contains 384 short- and long-term recommendations of various degrees of complexity. Indicated in an annex, the least of those that in the view of the experts, should be tackled as a matter of priority. As mandated, the experts made recommendations related to issues and the three main clusters: governance, the judiciary, and the proceedings. I stress the holistic and fundamental nature of many of the recommendations that do not only relate to specific issues of structure and decision making, or the legal and technical intricacies of the criminal proceedings. Indeed the experts have gone further to touch upon matters that affect the soul of the system, such as ethics at the court, as well as its culture and working environment, conflict of interest, and conflict prevention and resolution at the court. Some of their recommendations aimed at strengthening cohesion, including by encouraging to go further and deeper in some of the initiatives already taken at the court, to allow for a more collegial judicial approach and more coherence and predictability of the jurisprudence. There are also recommendations to the Assembly of State Parties itself, including to improve the process of nomination and selection of judges. This is in my view a hugely important and urgent matter. After all, the court, as any other institution, can only be as good as the men and women that work there.

Upon reception of the report, the Assembly of State Parties established a review mechanism to assess and implement the recommendations as appropriate through an inclusive and transparent dialogue open to all — the court, the assembly, civil society organizations, and all other relevant stakeholders of the international community. This will be done in accordance with the comprehensive plan of action that details the roadmap to be followed within a tight and ambitious timeline. Discussions have already started this month with a view to presenting a first report to the assembly at this December's incoming session at The Hague. When I assumed the position of the President of the Assembly of State Parties in February of this year, I emphasized the crucial importance and urgency of this review. This is an absolute top priority for the assembly and for me personally, as I am convinced, like my four predecessors in their letter, that a profound revision of the system is indeed required for the court to be able to deliver on its crucial justice message.

On 17 July, 1998, the international community materialized an idea whose time had come. Driven by a belief that accountability for the most serious crimes was indispensable to attain sustainable peace, and the conviction that a permanent general court had a central role to play in this regard. At the time of an erosion of the rule of law, and taking into account the contemporary challenges to multilateral solutions, an effective court is more important than ever. For this reason, I intend to do my utmost from my current position to contribute to enhance its effectiveness, its credibility, and its relevance. I thank you for your attention

2021 Academic Symposium Transcript

Inamori Ethics Prize Academic Symposium and Cox International Law Center Conference: Human Rights and International Law

Judge Silvia Fernández de Gurmendi
International Criminal Court judge; advocate for international justice, humanitarian law, and human rights; and recipient of the 2020 Inamori Ethics Prize, awarded in 2021
Shannon French
Inamori Professor in Ethics and Director of the Inamori International Center for Ethics and Excellence
Michael Scharf
Joseph C. Hostetler—BakerHostetler Professor of Law and Co-Dean of the CWRU School of Law
Jessica Wolfendale
Professor of Philosophy, Marquette University

TRECASA: Good afternoon and welcome. I'm Beth Trecasa. I'm the associate director of the Inamori International Center for Ethics and Excellence. It is my honor to address everyone here today as well as those of you who are watching us online. As many of you know, this event has been nearly two years in the making and represents the culmination of the Inamori Center's Conversations on Justice. Before we begin today's symposium, I'd like to ask you to join me in a moment of silence, a moment of sadness, to reflect on injustices everywhere—in our own neighborhoods in Northeast Ohio, across these United States, and across the world. So let us pause, recognize this momentary peace, before we must return to whatever injustices we are personally and professionally fighting. Thank you. It is my honor to introduce you to Provost Ben Vinson and to the Inamori Ethics Prize Academic Symposium and the beginning of the Cox Law Center Conference. Thank you.

VINSON: Beth, thank you so much for that. Good afternoon everyone, honored guests. I am Ben Vinson, the Provost and Executive Vice President of Case Western Reserve University. It is my pleasure to open the 2021 Inamori Ethics Prize Academic Symposium. Joining me on stage today are Judge Silvia Fernández de Gurmendi, advocate for human rights and international law, and recipient of our 2020 Inamori Ethics Prize; Professor Shannon French, the Inamori Professor in Ethics and the director of the Inamori International Center for Ethics and Excellence; Professor Michael Scharf, co-dean of our law school and the Joseph C. Baker Hostetler Professor of Law; And finally, Professor Jessica Wolfendale, chair and professor of philosophy at Marquette University and an international scholar in military ethics. Everyone please join me in welcoming our panelists. *[applause]* We are here today because of the vision and generosity of Dr. Kazuo Inamori and the Inamori Foundation. Their endowment created both the Inamori International Center for Ethics and Excellence and the annual Inamori Ethics Prize. I would also like to recognize donors and community partners for their support, whether they are in the audience today or watching online. They include: the Callahan Foundation, especially the Vice Chair of our Board of Trustees, Tim Callahan and his wife, Nancy, who are dear and longtime friends and champions of this university; Meredith Cycle; the Marshall and Yuko Hung Foundation; Etan Corporation; Quality Electrodynamics Corporation (QED); Third Federal Foundation, and Underwriter's Laboratories (UL). We thank you, and all Inamori Center Advisory Board members, for helping us continue our tradition of honoring global ethical leadership. We are delighted to have a live audience with us today—this means a lot for us here at this institution—and we also want to offer a special welcome to everyone who is watching online via livestream. This includes students from several local high schools, and from Case Western Reserve's own Global Ethical Leaders Society, and a number of our SAGES classes. Thank you so much for being a part of today's events!

So we want to get into our conversation as quickly as we can, but first let me tell you a bit about our panelists. Beginning with our 2020 Ethics Prize Honoree, Judge Silvia Fernández de Gurmendi. Judge Fernández is a leading force for international justice and has twenty years of experience in the practice of international law, humanitarian law, and human rights. She played a central role in the creation of the International Criminal Court (the ICC) and has worked tirelessly to see that those who commit war crimes and crimes against humanity are held accountable. She was also the first woman to serve as President of the ICC and is a champion of gender parity in international law. Before joining the ICC, Judge Fernández was Director General for Human Rights at the Ministry of Foreign Affairs in Argentina. She also represented Argentina before other human rights bodies, and she advised on issues related to the prevention of genocide and other atrocities. We are absolutely thrilled to have Judge Fernández with us today.

Now, joining Judge Fernández on our panel are our other two distinguished guests, Michael Scharf—Michael Scharf has been co-dean of Case Western Reserve University's School of Law since 2013; again, he is the Joseph C. Baker Hostetler Professor of Law and serves as managing director of the Nobel Peace Prize-nominated Public International Law and Policy Group. He has led transitional justice projects in Uganda, Côte d'Ivoire, Libya, Turkey, and maritime piracy projects in Kenya, Mauritius, and the Seychelles. In 2008, Scharf served as Special Assistant to the Prosecutor of the Cambodia Genocide tribunal. During the elder Bush and Clinton administrations, he served in the office of the legal advisor of the US Department of State. Scharf is the author of over one hundred scholarly articles and twenty books, four of which have won national book awards.

Professor Jessica Wolfendale—her primary research focuses on the ethics of political violence and the moral psychology of state-sponsored violence. She is the author of the books *War Crimes: Causes, Excuses, and Blame*, as well as *Torture and the Military Profession*. She has also published a number of articles and books on terrorism, the ethics of torture, security, military ethics, and war crimes. She is currently working on a new book project on the toleration of torture and terrorism in America. You can read more about our panelists on the Inamori Center website. Now, I look forward to hearing your conversation, and I hope all of you will take this opportunity to listen and to engage with our panelists. So let me turn it over now to Dr. Shannon French, the Inamori Professor of Ethics, who will moderate today's special panel presentation. Thank you. *[applause]*

FRENCH: In this world I have to remember to take off my mask so you all can hear me! Thank you all for being here and thank you, Provost Vinson for that lovely introduction. As you heard, the topic of today's conversation is human rights and international law, and this panel is both the academic symposium for the Inamori Ethics prize and also the opening event for the Cox International Law Center's annual conference, which will also continue all day tomorrow. And I should note that this year's conference is celebrating the thirtieth anniversary of the Cox International Law Center. I will be using my privilege as moderator to open with some questions of my own, but as I imagine you've noticed, there are some microphones—I feel like a flight attendant—there are microphones in the aisles on either side of you. I will ask some questions and get the conversation rolling but as I'm doing that, as our speakers are speaking, please feel free to be formulating your own questions and then form orderly queues behind those mics and we will do our best to get to some of your questions in the time that we have. I say some, because this is my thirteenth academic symposium, and we have yet to get through every question that is available, but we will do our best. So to start us out, I'm going to open with you Dean Scharf, if I may. Michael, given your extensive experience with the struggle to hold accountable those who commit crimes against humanity, can you help put our conversation today in context? Why has Silvia's work been so important to Human Rights and why is an entity like the ICC necessary?

SCHARF: That's a great question to start out with. You know, despite the developments of the law of war, the genocide convention, and the human rights treaties, the last hundred years and even the last fifty years have been the bloodiest in the history of humankind. If you think back to the eve of World War II, right after Hitler assembled his generals and told them that they were going to invade Poland in 1939, and they were going to have total war and they were going to do things that had never been done before, including having mobile death squads. The German generals were squeamish about this, and they weren't sure that that was something they wanted to sign up for. And Hitler said to them: "Don't worry. Who after all remembers the fate of the Armenians?" And what he was talking about was the fact that during World War I, the first genocide in modern times was the Turks against the Armenians, and instead of holding anybody accountable, there was a Treaty of Lausanne that gave amnesty to all the responsible Turkish leaders. And that told Hitler that if we win the war, we too will get away with it. Even if we lose the war, because Turkey lost the war, we'll get away with it, and the German generals then marched happily on, and you know the rest is history. Well, after Nuremberg, there was some hope that there was going to be a permanent International Criminal Court to hold people responsible like they held the Nazis at that first international tribunal, but that was not to happen because of the Cold War, it was a golden age of impunity. The UN Human Rights repertoire said it was such a bad time that a person stood a better chance of being prosecuted for killing one person or ten people than for killing ten thousand or a hundred thousand. It was a time when we saw atrocities committed in Cambodia and Iraq, in Uganda, in Latin America, and throughout the world, and nobody even talked about prosecutions. Well that started to change in 1993 when genocide returned to Europe, and the International

Community created the Yugoslavia tribunal, followed a year later by the creation of the Rwanda tribunal. And after a slow start, where at first the NATO troops refused to arrest any war criminals even when they came by the checkpoints and they knew who they were, things started to change. They got with it. And now, every single indicted person from the Yugoslavia tribunal, and just about everyone from the Rwanda tribunal who survived has been brought to justice. Now some of them were acquitted, but many of them were convicted and that's also a sign of international justice—when there are fair trials and people can be acquitted. Now that led to the creation of the Special Court for Sierra Leone, and by the way, the Chief Prosecutor for the Special Court for Sierra Leone is in this room today: Jim Johnson—a little shout out! *[applause]*

It led to the creation of the Cambodia tribunal, the Special Tribunal for Lebanon, and ultimately the International Criminal Court. Judge Fernández was on the ground floor of the creation of the permanent International Criminal Court. She played a lead role in the negotiations. Then, she was elected as one of the first judges— she was elected president of the International Criminal Court, an incredibly powerful, important position. She had courageous decisions, including some great dissents, that I think in the future will become majority opinions, and now she is the president of the Assembly of State Parties. The ICC has been around now for twenty years—it's leaving its fledgling period, and it's entering its adolescence. It's maturing, if you think about some of your kids if you have any, or some of you are just in your twenties. That's the ICC, and it's got a long history ahead of it as well. It has prosecuted some major cases, but it has failed to get custody over some of the major indicted war criminals. So, for example, al-Bashir, who's wanted for genocide for the Darfur conflict, he's been hopscotching around—not just the Middle East, but Africa, and even China. And not one country that is party to the ICC—those countries that are party of the Assembly of State Parties—ever arrested him. Now, he's just fallen from power, he's under house arrest, maybe things will change, but he's still not at the Hague. And then you have Saif Gaddafi, the son of Muammar Gaddafi. He's still in Libya, hasn't been surrendered. And then you've got Joseph Kony, the head of the Lord's Resistance Army, who kidnapped sixty thousand children and turned them into sex slaves and child soldiers, and he's still on the loose. So, the ICC has incredible challenges ahead of it, but Judge Fernández is the political face of the ICC. Those challenges fall on, now, at her doorstep, and it's a huge, huge, job for her to play. She has to convince the state parties to comply with the arrest warrants, which is not going to be easy, as the al-Bashir case shows. She has to convince them not to withdraw from the ICC—many of the countries in Africa have questioned whether the ICC is just focused on Africa unfairly, and have threatened to withdraw, and there is a very, very difficult dance going on right now, politically, that Judge Fernández will find herself in the middle of. And of course, she has to convince them to keep the financing flowing, which is always difficult, especially during a pandemic.

So, the question is: What is the importance of the ICC? Its importance is to stop the age of impunity and bring accountability, and some deterrence. And who has the most important role to play? I think, arguably, she is sitting right next to me.

FRENCH: *[laughter]* Well, you know, no pressure Silvia! Given what Professor Scharf just said, and what you spoke of last night in your wonderful remarks where you told us the three-act story of how we got to where we are now—can you help us understand why it is that some countries, including the United States, remain uncomfortable with the existence of the ICC and reluctant to affirm the jurisdiction of the ICC?

FERNÁNDEZ: Thank you, thank you very much, good afternoon to you all. It is really a great pleasure to be with this fantastic panel discussing these issues with you. Thank you for the pressure and let's start by trying to give a few answers to your specific question.

Why some countries are reluctant, including the United States, but not only. Let's start by recalling that, at this point in time, 123 states have joined the ICC, the Rome Statute: the founding treaty of the court. 123 states is not insignificant; it's almost two-thirds of the international community. For a relatively young and complex institution, this is quite an achievement. But that means that around seventy states remain outside the court. So, among these seventy, you have different reasons and even no reasons. I would say that you would have a category of states that are reluctant to join because they fear—and I would say this in very broad terms—they would fear an overreach of internationalism against national sovereignty, overreach, excess of internationalism, and a desire to keep certain decisions on who is going to be investigated and prosecuted to remain national decisions, without any kind of international intervention. In this regard, it is important to recall that the court is indeed a last resort institution. It's not intended and has not been created to step in and start investigating and prosecuting in states. On the contrary, it's based on the idea that the best solution is national prosecutions and investigations. But it's also based on the idea that certain crimes cannot be left exclusively to the decisions of states because they are crimes that affect international society as a whole, and that is why when states do not wish, or are not able for whatever reasons, to investigate and prosecute, then it is for international institutions to step in. But some states are reluctant to this idea and prefer to keep these decisions for themselves, and some big countries with global responsibilities fear this excess of internationalism most. But then there are the other states that have other reasons, or no reasons, I would say. Some say: "What is for me here? Why should I join this institution?" Because it creates some obligations: you need to cooperate, you need to pay contributions, and actually the ratification and implementation nationally is burdensome, in a way. So they see "there is nothing here for me, we have other priorities." And then there are others that have specific, constitutional issues that they feel are too complicated to solve, and it's not their priority. Some have changed their constitutions in order to ratify the Rome Statute because, among other important provisions, the Rome Statute, the treaty, doesn't allow for immunities. So, some countries have tried, have modified their constitutions in order to be able to join. France, among others, has changed their constitutions, Colombia, in Latin America. Sometimes this is a very easy change, but it needs to go through the process. So you have different reasons there, and these reasons need to be addressed in various and different ways, but maybe we can come to that later. And I would say at the end that another reason is also that the concept of a permanent court has created overwhelming enthusiasm in the past, but then the institution has also grown into creating some dissatisfaction, disappointment in some quarters, saying, "Well, this court is too focused on Africa," or "This court is too slow," or "This court is too inefficient," so that also adds to some reluctancy. So, that's why I say that we need to look into each one of these categories of arguments and address them in a different way in order to persuade more states to join.

FRENCH: I find that very helpful to be reminded that there isn't one answer to that question that, indeed, as you say, we may end up with seventy different reasons why they won't agree to it. I'd like to turn to you, Jessica, now, and we've heard several times now this talk of the end of the age of impunity. As your excellent scholarship shows, preventing war crimes and atrocities is a very complex endeavor with many layers to it. And so I wonder if you could comment on what you see as the importance of legal accountability in that effort, such as what the ICC hopes to provide. How meaningful is it?

WOLFENDALE: Thank You. First of all, I would just like to say it's a real honor to be on a panel with Dean Scharf and Judge Fernández. And what I'm going to say really is, I'm not an expert in legal accountability, but what I think is very important in thinking about preventing war crimes is the way legal accountability is communicative. Right, so particularly at the global stage. So it communicates something about a condemnation of the crime that is being punished. And even the creation of, or the labeling of, a particular act as a crime is already itself a form of condemnation. And then if someone is specifically punished, that further emphasizes the idea that this crime is something which is taken seriously. And that is crucially important for a number of reasons. One, I think, it gives voice to the victims in a way which I think really needs to be centralized when thinking about how we deal with war crimes in prioritizing the victims first and foremost. What it can do, for example, is give voice to victims whose suffering has not so far been codified as a crime. And I think Judge Fernández has done amazing work on this in relation to sexual violence and conflict, which I believe wasn't actually a war crime until the Rome Statues or even after that. So just by naming something as a crime itself, shows a measure of respect and recognition for the victims who have suffered that crime. And that's extremely important in and of itself even if the actual trials of the people accused of those crimes may or may not result in convictions. I'm less convinced that punishment at the international level acts as a deterrent because, often, it can be the case that, particularly with large-scale war crimes, those involved don't see what they are doing as a crime. So they're not going to be deterred by people who are punished for war crimes if they don't think that what they are doing is a crime. And, and so that's, I think, why punishment at the international level as communicative better captures what accountability at that level can do and can do specifically for victims. I think that there are limits to legal accountability, and some of them are just inherent to the nature of legal accountability. So these aren't intended to be criticisms so much as a recognition that legal accountability can really only do so much. So first of all, legal accountability—and we've seen this with the trials that the ICC has dealt with—is a matter primarily of individual accountability. So as an individual is held morally and legally responsible, in this case, for specific crimes, but in many of the crimes that we are concerned with on this panel such as genocide or institutionalized torture, the responsibility for those crimes rests on hundreds, even thousands of individuals who are involved at different levels. And there's just no way that any system of legal accountability can adequately accommodate that idea of shared or collective responsibility. So that's just a limitation of the legal system, right? Again, it's not intended to be a criticism, instead it's to show that when you're thinking about accountability for war crimes, we have to think of legal accountability as only one kind. That, if there is to be true change, and, again, true acknowledgment of the harm of war crimes, we have to think of other mechanisms for accountability. So, this is where, for example, truth and reconciliation might play a role in that, right?

Another limitation, I think, is that the kind of responsibility that legal accountability is interested in is backward-looking. It's punishing someone for what they have done in the past, and that's completely appropriate. Again, this is not a criticism, it's just the nature of legal accountability in general. It's to do with the function of blame—someone is punished for something they've done in the past—they're blamed for it, they're held morally responsible for it. But there's nothing in that concept of responsibility that's essentially forward-looking, that talks about a duty, looking forward, to say, prevent or change the circumstances that might lead to further instances of that crime, and some philosophers have talked about the difference between sort of forward-looking and backward-looking responsibility in terms of whether or not blame is involved. So, you might, for example, think that a state or a society or citizens might bear forward-looking responsibility without being blameworthy, perhaps, because they have benefited from injustice or benefited, in some way, from war crimes, even unintentionally. So, that sense of bearing a kind of shared responsibility that's disconnected from blame, I think, is a very valuable idea in thinking about how societies might take steps—whether it's through, again, things like truth and reconciliation commissions, through change in political procedures, even just through speaking out about certain events— to address that idea: "well maybe there's some shared forward-looking responsibility here" to try and recognize and address the injustice of war crimes and to take steps to prevent it. So that's again just a limitation of the legal system in general in terms of how effective it can be, ultimately, in helping prevent war crimes.

I also think, too—and this occurred to me while listening to Dean Scharf talk—that the language we use in relation to accountability also shapes our moral understanding of what was done, and for, which we hold people—the actions for which we hold people accountable. So, thinking about genocide, so

Dean Scharf talked about the twentieth century as being one of the bloodiest centuries, and genocide, and the Armenian Genocide being one of the first genocides of the modern world. Now, that's true if we think only in terms of if we exclude, for example, the genocide of indigenous peoples through colonization, right? So the language that we use to talk about war crimes itself shapes our moral understanding of what counts as a war crime, and whose voices matter when we think about accountability? So, for example, if we reserve our thinking about war crimes, and I'm talking here beyond the scope of legal accountability, of course, two cases, the primary cases from the twentieth century, and we neglect to think, for example, of the extraordinary violence inflicted on indigenous peoples. That again, and I'm not saying this is an intentional effect, but it does have the effect of marginalizing certain kinds of voices and prioritizing others. So, and I think the law, again, the language we use in relation to legal accountability, more broadly, has that effect. Even in terms of the language we use to talk about what is a crime, and how much punishment certain crimes deserve. So people have often talked about, for example, that, in domestic society, not just on the international stage, degrees of punishment reflect attitudes about how seriously harm inflicted by harm—by an act—might be. And we've often seen cases where, for example, sexual violence is punished less severely than, I don't know, breaking and entering, right? And that tells us something about the relative value accorded to the victims of those crimes, and how seriously the harm against them is taken, and I think that also might be true at the international stage, right, that they could be and, again, here I'd defer to the experts on the International Criminal Court on this panel, but again, the kind of punishments that are given for different crimes are also communicative, along with the fact that something has been named a crime at all. I think I'll leave my comments there, and, again, I'm very grateful to be part of this discussion.

FRENCH: I think it's very vital that you remind us to take in the perspective of the victims and point out that the language that we use to describe and define some of these crimes allows some victims to feel seen and others to feel further marginalized. That's an incredibly important point, and actually Silvia, I'd like to connect that up to asking a question to you and then, Michael, if you'd like to weigh in after Silvia on this. So, when you spoke with us last October since you have been part of these conversations on justice now for two years, we talked about how the work of the ICC does depend on the idea that some notions of right and wrong are not culturally dependent, or not merely culturally dependent, that there are such things that can be called "crimes against humanity," again the language being so important here, and that that can be true wherever and, to Jessica's point, whenever they occur. So, looking further back in history, we can say that was also a genocide, that was also a crime against humanity. From your experience, can you tell us more about why this concept of universal human rights is vital for global stability, and if you'd like to tie that to Jessica's comments about the victims, feel free.

FERNÁNDEZ: Thank you, thank you very much. Wow, there is so much in this question. Really, because there are so many angles, but the concept that there are some common universal standards is essential to start the conversation. And actually yesterday, when we explained the process of creation of the international criminal court, I went into the details on how we identified and agreed on these common standards for the purpose of international criminal justice. Now I would like to go back to what Michael Scharf said. Michael mentioned that the Cold War had been the golden age for impunity. And I fully agree with that, but at the same time they were not lost years, because they were also years that were extremely fertile in the setting of standards. And a setting of standards that have now, if not unanimous, very broad support. And I'm talking in the humanitarian sphere, you have the Geneva Conventions, you have, in the human rights area, the International Covenants for Civil and Political Rights and Economic and Cultural Rights, you have the Genocide Convention, the Torture Convention. So all these conventions are extremely important in the setting of standards that the broad international community, to call it somehow, or international society, have agreed to.

Now the discrepancies start at the point when you want to enforce these standards. And that has been the huge problem and that's why it is not incompatible to have a golden age for no standard setting while you have a golden age for impunity. The discussions start when you need to enforce them, and also that is what also undermines stability. And that's why the tribunals and the International Criminal Court were created on the assumption that you need to enforce those standards because justice is a component, and an essential component, of sustainable peace. So you will not have stability if you continue having just impunity. So when you mention something to be a crime and you said, crimes against humanity, crimes against humanity. Yes, you are going into this fear of enforcement. This is not just about violation of human rights. We are talking about something that is so egregious, is such a gross violation, that deserves to be punished and individuals deserve to be punished, so we go into enforcement. So that's why, what has been extremely important in the concept of accountability is that it has added this enforcement, this teeth to the setting, to these standards. So this, I think, continues to be crucial for the stability of the actual enforcement of all these norms and standards that we have identified. So I do believe that some of these standards are really universally agreed to. I don't think anybody, maybe very marginally, would say that crimes against humanity are good or that it is okay to torture. But actually, in practice, you may have circumstances where some things are going to be either denied or defended in light of the circumstances. That's why I think accountability continues to be the extra component that was required for stability. And I quote the secretary general when he said where international accountability for these crimes is indeed the greatest achievements of the last three decades for the rule of law.

FRENCH: Michael, please join this conversation

SCHARF: So let me begin with what you asked and tie it into what both of my colleagues have been talking about. And some background first, so in general human rights law there are some concepts like cultural relativism and the margin of appreciation doctrine. These were necessary because in order to get all the countries of the world to join in on a uniform set of standards for human rights, it had to be watered down, and there were compromises made. And so cultural relativism says that in interpreting these very general squishy words, you have to look at the history and the culture of each country. And the margin of appreciation doctrine says you have to be deferential to the way that countries' courts, organizations, executive branch, officials, interpret their own laws. Now those do not have any place in international criminal law. These crimes have now been codified in treaties and in the statutes of the international tribunals. There is now more precedent on these crimes, defining them in specific terms, than in any other area of international law. And there are rules like the Latin phrase "nellum crimean cine leger" which is basically the American version of the ex post facto prohibition that says you cannot prosecute people for crimes that were not defined at the time they committed them. Now that answers Professor Wolfendale's question about the indigenous people. These treaties, these body of laws, didn't exist when the United States was marching Manifest Destiny across the continent and committing what would be genocide today. But there was no Genocide Convention, there was no definition of a crime at that point and the same with the Australian indigenous peoples. Horrible things, but we're often asked, well, why aren't they prosecuted by the ICC? And that's because international criminal law has this ex post facto prohibition; you can only move forward and not look back. And that also was a compromise because otherwise the countries in the world were not going to sign up to a treaty that would open up a thousand years of their actions. So they got a clean slate for everything that occurred before 2002; that was the essential compromise. But I think that you know answers to the question you are asking, and it addresses sort of some of what you were saying.

WOLFENDALE: That's a good point, but I guess my point wasn't so much about the existence of treaties because, of course, that's absolutely right, but just that when we talk about a concept like genocide, which is now used in a context outside of the strict application of international law, using that language is still valuable for capturing the moral depth of harm that was committed prior to the existence of these treaties. Even, if it doesn't mean that therefore there should be legal accountability in that case because that was the ex post facto rule (I know some Latin, but it's all like philosophy Latin, so not Latin). So that's right, but again, when we talk about this, and use these concepts, expanding them outside that street context, it is important to think about when we use that word to apply what was happening to indigenous people, we are we're not saying necessarily and therefore there should be legal accountability. What we're saying is that what was them what was done to them reaches the scale of the harm of the cases that are covered by the treaty. So that's still very important. And I think another factor and again this is what's talking about legal accountability, is just really being one relatively narrow form of accountability, although extremely important I should add, is that recognizing the way in which the harm of these previously unrecognized atrocities continues well into the twentieth century, as we've seen with the mass graves uncovered at the Canadian residential schools recently. And I think indigenous activists wouldn't try to make this point is that it's not as if this was an isolated crime that occurred three hundred years ago and then everything's been okay since. Like the ramifications are ongoing and some of the practices involved with aspects of genocide are still in some senses ongoing. And so that does raise a specter, and again, I'm not arguing that therefore the International Criminal Court should be involved, but it does raise the aspect of the thought: Well okay if there are aspects of this crime that's still ongoing maybe this does fall into the purview of at least some kinds of legal accountability. But that's as much as I would be able to say about that in terms of details.

FRENCH: In these conversations to include the explanation and the detail that we got last night from you, Silvia, and then what you were adding to our understanding there, Michael, about the ex post facto as it were because I think there will be people who will want to dismiss the efforts, today, of the of international law because they will see them as having missed all these previous crimes. And it's helpful to say they weren't missed, this was not in any way being dismissive; it was, as you called it, a compromise that had to be made to move forward at all. I'm also reminded, I don't know the source, but our dean of the college, Dean Ward, used a phrase last night when we were discussing these same things where she said that "there is no new evil in the world." That she had heard that quote and that that point seems to ring through all of your comments as well that each of these past acts, no matter how far you go, does have follow-on harms and follow-on damage to people who are still alive today, and yet there are legal limits to how that can be carried out. I of course have more questions because I love talking about this, but I did want to remind you all that, if you want to ask questions, this is your cue, now is your time, it's your cue to queue, it's your opportunity to come to the microphone and form a small line. Don't be scared, and I will continue with my questions until questioners appear there. With that, I have a kind of a general thing I want to ask to all three of you, so you can think about who wants to jump in first. But certainly this has been on my mind and I know it's been on many people's minds that there have been so many cycles of bleak, discouraging news from around the world lately. This this includes everything from the pandemic, to climate disasters, to starvation in Yemen, to re-education camps for Uighurs, to the Rohingya massacres, slaughter and sexual violence in Tigre, and we, just this month, passed the grim milestone of twenty years since the attacks of 9/11 and the ragged ends of what were previously termed the forever wars that followed those attacks. So what I would like, and I'm almost pleading with the three of you here, is for me and for members of the audience who are looking for a bit of hope or optimism about the human race, can you please share any signs you've seen of positive moral progress improving the condition of humankind? All right, thank you! Give us some hope, Michael.

SCHARF: I'm a bit of an optimist. Often people know that my specialty is genocide, crimes against humanity, and I smile a lot—I'm a very upbeat person, and they're like, "How can you do that?" And I am a bit of an optimist—I think that every single time there is a success story we're getting closer to, you know, resolving these problems—to a world where they're less. So I would say there's sort of a Kantian march forward but, if you graphed it, it wouldn't be a straight line. It'd be more like a bull market in the United States Stock Exchange so it kind of goes up and down, up and down, but there is positive forward movement, and it's also related to what Professor Wolfendale was saying about the commutative value of this exercise. So what you notice is that the ICC is now appearing more and more frequently in movies, and on TV shows— there is a current TV show dedicated to the ICC—its investigations are very public before they are even to the stage of confirmation of arrest warrants just when they launch an investigation.

FRENCH: It's not *Law and Order: ICC*, is it?

SCHARF: Yeah, ICC, that'd be the next one. But the investigations, every once in a while, the prosecutor will have a press conference when she or he finds out that there is a major crisis brewing and there's a concern that there's going to be a genocide. There's even organizations like the Genocide and Holocaust Museum in Washington that has this chart of genocide warnings, and it rates each country around the world with different colors as they're concerned that there might be a genocide problem—and this goes for crimes against humanity and war crimes as well. So, when the prosecutor says: "I am investigating," we have seen examples where things dampen down very quickly. There is concern, people are starting to learn, and I agree with Professor Wolfendale—the leaders, they don't really do a logical cost-benefit analysis. But, it is the generals, the colonels, the lieutenants, that—and this is what you teach—they do. They care very much about the laws of war. They're taught about the laws of war and they're very concerned that they might be prosecuted and so what we find is that international justice is patient and persistent. Think about in here, in Ohio, there was this guy named John Demjanjuk. He was this auto worker that was very well liked in Ohio, but it turned out that he was a concentration camp guard at one of the most notorious concentration camps, and when the information came out there was a very well-publicized extradition case and he went to Germany at age ninety-two; and there was a question: Why would you want to prosecute an old guy who spent the entire life redeeming himself, showing that he had been rehabilitated, showing that when he's not in a war he's a good guy, and the answer is because international justice must be patient and persistent. You must never be able to get away with it. That's part of the story that's communicated. So, you think about, you know, Cambodia, it took thirty years after the Killing Fields for people to be prosecuted. Iraq: Saddam Hussein got away with it for twenty years before he fell from power and was prosecuted by a quasi-international court with judges from his own country, and I will return to the story that I began with Al-Bashir. He thought he was getting away with it, but he fell from power, he's in custody, there are negotiations right now. If he is surrendered to the ICC, I believe this will be the most important case of its young life. It will show that a president of a country that committed genocide and got away with it finally was surrendered and that international justice prevailed, but it took a long time. But, again, the story is international justice is persistent and patient, and that is what educates people. That is the message, I think, and that's a positive message.

FRENCH: It is a positive message, and I like those words: patient and persistent. We're going to hear now some more from Silvia and Jessica but, delightfully, we have lines, and so as soon as you have each commented on this point, I will go ahead and open the floor. So, please take it away, Silvia!

FERNÁNDEZ: Ok, then I will be very brief, because I see the line there, that is great we get to engage with you, but I just wanted to add to what Michael has said and also Jessica, also on a positive note, because I'm also an optimist. But indeed, we see huge, horrendous atrocities being committed around us. We see more crises than ever around us now, and you say: "What have we done, have we made any progress?" Well I do think that the difference from now and before is that, probably, now there is more hope for justice, for victims, than ever before. We have left these golden ages of impunity and we go into an age of accountability. That doesn't mean that everybody's accountable, of course not, but now there is a hope that there will be accountability, and there is an expectation that there will be accountability, even when, for whatever reasons, there is no tribunal to deal with the matter, like, for instance, the ICC, because it has no jurisdiction for certain cases or situations. Then, there is [that the] international community creates mechanisms to safeguard the evidence, collect the evidence, give it to national prosecutors, give it to anybody who will deal with this. So there is this expectation that certain acts, certain crimes, cannot go unpunished. So, if it is not now, it will be later, but there will be justice, so I think this is a huge step forward.

FRENCH: That is hopeful, and I will note that right here at Case Western we're doing some of that work, including things like the Yemen Project, is that correct? Actually gathering that evidence—

SCHARF: I mentioned Jim Johnson, the prosecutor from the Special Court for Sierra Leone. He is a professor at the Law School, and he has seventy-five law students working around the clock developing case files for some day, when the political winds are in the right direction, that there can be a prosecution for what are horrendous war crimes and crimes against humanity in Yemen. Right now, because Saudi Arabia is involved and because Saudi Arabia is very economically and politically powerful and has a lot of great friends, including the United States, nobody is trying to prosecute that. So, if you just looked at a snapshot, you would be very pessimistic. But if you met Jim Johnson and his students—they're preparing for the future day when the winds will change and their work will lead to the successful prosecution of these people.

FRENCH: Jessica?

WOLFENDALE: I'm going to start with a lot of pessimism—

FRENCH: *[laughter]*

WOLFENDALE: I wrote a paper recently about the erasure of torture in American history and the long history of the failure of successive American administrations to hold anyone accountable for torture. Not just the recent post-9/11 torture program, which, at least in relation to my students, most of my students have never heard of it, but also historically in relation to the use of torture, for example, by US forces in the Philippines at the turn of the early—the end of the nineteenth, turn of the twentieth century. Again, even though there was public knowledge there, nobody was held accountable at that time. So for me, researching that article was quite depressing. This ongoing pattern of the use of torture, then the failure of any kind of reasonable form of accountability, and then the kind of erasure of the torture from public and political consciousness, but here's the little bit of optimism. I've been watching *Ted Lasso*, which makes me feel optimistic, but that's bit of a different point. But, I think what we are seeing, at least in America, not so much in Australia unfortunately, is the beginnings of a reckoning with American history, and this is through conversations about Confederate monuments, the Black Lives Matter movement, the #MeToo movement, so, slowly, slowly, I think that marginalized voices have been a little bit more visible than they used to be.

Unfortunately, there's been quite a significant backlash against both of those movements and, I think the move to ban Critical Race Theory is just the latest example of this. But the existence of the backlash itself tells us, in a sense, about the greater visibility of these voices of previously marginalized groups, and so that is something to be slightly optimistic about; so, not quite the, glowing scale—we're making progress, but I think that is something to be hopeful about.

FRENCH: It is, it is. So, we are now entering what I like to think of as the lightning round. So, we are going to have to go fairly quickly, and so, I will warn our questioners that we will not have any "this is more of a comment" but, you need to come at us with a question and then we will pop it over to our panel. Let us start—Ben! Let's—go right ahead! *[laughter]* I just saw you there.

VINSON: I just was wondering: the pandemic has changed so much in our world. Has it really changed the work of the ICC in any way, and wonder if you could talk about that.

FRENCH: That seems to you, Silvia!

FERNÁNDEZ: Thank you, thank you for this. Actually we have been all praising how resilient the court has been during the pandemic, because they managed to continue with their proceedings. Of course, they changed very much and they had to adapt, and only a few people were allowed to be at the seat of the court, just those who were absolutely necessary to support the proceedings, which were mainly done through digital means. A lot of witness taken—that had already started even before the pandemic, lots of digital technology being used. But, they were very creative, very imaginative, and indeed, it has been praised and, during the last assembly, we really praised the court for managing to go forward to the extent that I also participated recently in a meeting with the Chief Justice of Jamaica, because they had asked for the support of the ICC to tell them their experience in this online virtual proceedings because they did extremely well, and also some Dutch tribunals also asked for the support of the ICC. So, of course, investigations have been very difficult, but everything continued. So, in that aspect, I really have to say that the court was extremely resilient, creative, and imaginative. So, good story, positive notes. *[laughter]*

FRENCH: It is! That followed on more smoothly than we might have—

SCHARF: Can I just add—

FRENCH: Yeah.

SCHARF: —even the International Criminal Court Moot Court Competition, which the ICC helps run, and which we are involved in, has been remote, and we had the argument in their courtroom, but they were able to do that, but in the preliminary rounds they used their technology to beam it in, and just as a little aside, our Law School was the runner-up in that competition. So that was a good year for us.

FRENCH: *[laughter]* That's fantastic! Ryan, over here! Oh, and introduce yourself quickly.

RYAN ARVIZU: Hi, my name is Ryan Arvizu. I am a graduate student here studying Military Ethics under Dr. French in the MA program. So, because I'm a student of philosophy, Professor Wolfendale, my question is more towards you and the war crimes that come out of active-duty military personnel. So you talk about, in your work, how these aren't failures, individual moral failures, but rather a military authoritarian culture that fails to establish that strong ethical base for its personnel. That does not justify war crimes, so I'm wondering, either through legal accountability or another method, how do we, especially as civilians, apply pressure to state-run militaries to change, and what do those changes look like in a practical manner? Thank you.

WOLFENDALE: Thank you for that question! So, my coauthor Matthew Talbot and I, in our book on war crimes, look into this question, and one of the things that we push back on is the common depiction of war crimes, and I think this is often how war crimes are commonly talked about even within military academies, as being failures of character. Individuals who are overcome by rage or loss of self-control, and that certainly does describe some kinds of war crimes, but it certainly doesn't capture, for example, institutionalized torture, or, in many cases, genocide, which is often a process of explicit policy authorization, normalization, justification. So then how do we citizens, for example, have civilians put pressure on military academies to address those kinds of war crimes? I think, first and foremost, this is very complex. I think accountability is a big part of that. So, I already mentioned my slight despair at looking at the lack of accountability, for example, in relation to the post-9/11 torture program; some of which falls in the military, but not all of course in that case. But I think it's also about the stories that are told about war crimes within military academies need to own up to the fact that "good people" can commit war crimes and can think that war crimes are not crimes. They can think that something that is a war crime is, in fact, what's required of them. That it's maybe even consistent with military duty or virtue. Even that acknowledgment would go some way to actually sort of reckoning with how institutional structures and institutional stories about war crimes can themselves contribute to war crimes. So that's what I mean. That's something which as civilians it might be how to exert that pressure. I guess it's about talking about it. It's about having conversations. It's about, putting that narrative out there, encouraging as much as we can, and military officials, in my view, or the ones I've interacted with, are actually very interested in this. So, again, there's not necessarily resistance to this idea, but I think it goes against long-standing ways of approaching the question of war crimes in military training. So I think that just needs to be fundamentally altered. I thank you for your question.

FRENCH: Same experience; they're not reluctant to have these conversations. You just have to, but I love the phrase that you use, the institutional stories about war crimes and that's what we need to look at, that's incredibly powerful. All right, over here, and please briefly say who you are.

NATALIE EBERTS: Hi, my name is Natalie Eberts. I'm a second-year law student here at our Law School, and my question is to the panel, and it's about some of the topics that came up earlier such as forward-looking or prevention of crimes against humanity as well as a victim focus, and I'm wondering: Are there any efforts, or is there any potential to bring some of those to the court within the limits of it being a legal accountability institution and, perhaps, on that like, consulting with victims about how the prosecution goes forward, because I know sometimes there may be situations where victims have opinions about how that happens or whether it happens, as well as voluntary reconciliation process that victims may want to engage in. So those types of things—is there any space for that and, if not, where would be the space for those things? Thank you.

FRENCH: I think we, if one of you would like to volunteer to take that question. Do we have a—

SCHARF: I can start. So I think what you're asking, Natalie, is if some of the incidents that predated the jurisdictional threshold of the court can still be addressed by the international community, or did we make some deal with the devil when we created the court to just ignore them, and I think this is something that Professor Wolfendale was mentioning before and that is that the ICC is not the only accountability mechanism, and the world doesn't need and it isn't a one-size-fit-all kind of place. So there's all kinds of other accountability mechanisms. There's truth commissions, investigative commissions, ad hoc tribunals, domestic prosecutions, and I think that all those are still open for business for the prior, in a variety of ways, for the prior incidents, and there are victim groups that are coming together to try to bring that forward. I think there's someone in the audience, Professor Tim Webster, who's been doing a lot of writing about the crimes that Japan committed during World War II, especially in Korea, with the comfort women and everything. For years those were ignored, and then there are now victims groups that have come together that have coalesced, and now there are actual court cases where those are starting to be tried—this is seventy-five years later—so, you know, there is still hope for the past.

FRENCH: Yeah, I'd like to add a nice connection for us here with the Inamori Ethics Prize. Our 2014 Inamori Ethics Prize recipient, Dr. Denis Mukwege, who went on to win the 2018 Nobel Peace Prize, there was a story just yesterday that came out that he is currently calling for justice for victims and requesting an international tribunal to look into war crimes in the Democratic Republic of Congo. So, again, this work is ongoing and involving different mechanisms that exist as ways to respond. I think that we should probably keep going with questions. Although I know each of our panelists could say something about each of these questions, but let's get another one in the mix. Please go right ahead.

HAMAD: Hi, my name is Hamad. I'm a doctoral student at Emory University School of Law. First I just want to congratulate Professor Michael Scharf for celebrating the thirty-year anniversary. My question would be, perhaps, directed to Judge Silvia about the Al-Bashir case. At the beginning, Professor Michael Scharf just mentioned that he has been maneuvering over his arrest warrant with the assistance of some state parties. The question is—and have you seen that two months ago the Sudanese authorities passed a national bill to join the Rome Statute of the International Criminal Court. How would this affect the arrest warrant of Al-Bashir that was actually issued by the Security Council of the United Nations? Do you think that the job after joining the Rome Statute would affect the subject matter of this arrest warrant given that he was actually arrested or—the international community wanted to arrest him because of genocide crimes, essentially for genocide, but do you think that after joining the International Criminal Court would be a possible extension for other crimes?

FRENCH: Judge Fernández?

FERNÁNDEZ: Thank you, thank you very much. Well, it was mentioned here that we are all looking and following the developments in Sudan, which are extremely important for the situation at the court. You know, the situation of Sudan, Darfur, was referred to the International Criminal Court by the Security Council in 2005, and the court, not the Security Council but the court itself, issued arrest warrants against several individuals in Sudan for alleged crimes committed in Darfur, including against the then-president, Al-Bashir, and as it was recalled by Michael at the beginning of this panel, this indeed was extremely controversial, extremely controversial because Al-Bashir at the time, being a president of Sudan in the exercise of his functions, and there was a huge discussion on whether he had or not immunity and also there were controversies and also Sudan at the time, and I go to your question on ratification: they considered that they were not obliged because they were not parties to the Rome Treaty. So, this is all arguably good legally, but the political developments in Sudan and when—if they take the decision to ratify, that would be an extremely positive signal in terms of willing[ness] to cooperate with the court. Of course, they will need to still make a decision with relation to Al-Bashir and what they do with that, but, a ratification of the Rome Statute would be an extremely positive signal for the entire situation, and I think the court has been of the view that Sudan was obliged to cooperate in all cases regardless of whether or not they ratified the Rome Statute because of the Security Council referral, but the ratification would add a willingness to cooperate that has not been really present before. So yeah, it would be a very positive development.

SCHARF: Just to add to that, the Security Council refers the case, but then when Al-Bashir goes to all these different countries and they don't arrest them and the president of the ICC, and the president of the Assembly of State Parties, the prosecutor begged the Security Council to take action—the Security Council is paralyzed by the veto. Now, this is a little commercial for day two of this conference, I see Jennifer Trahan sitting in front of us. She has a wonderful book that has won awards, and she's going to be speaking about it tomorrow, the Security Council's paralysis is the biggest obstacle to the success of international justice, and she has recipes for circumventing that, and you have to come back tomorrow to hear more about that.

FRENCH: And a question over here please.

KAMAREA VALENTINE: Hi, my name is Kamarea Valentine and I'm a freshman here at Case Western, and I would like to congratulate Judge Fernández on her award, and my question is open to all the panelists. I just wanted to ask: How does the influence of white supremacy affect the lack of accountability in war crimes and genocide against BIPOC individuals by white communities and do we prioritize accountability of BIPOC states over predominantly white states because of their influence within the international community?

FRENCH: I'm so sorry but could you spell out—not everyone will know the acronym—

VALENTINE: Oh! yeah!

FRENCH: —and just for a moment, take off your mask because our mics are muffling you. I'm so sorry, it's not your fault!

VALENTINE: No, you're fine! BIPOC stands for Black, Indigenous, and People of Color.

FRENCH: And just restate the question with the mask down just so we can hear.

VALENTINE: So my question was: How does the influence of white supremacy affect the lack of accountability in war crimes and genocide against BIPOC individuals by white communities, and do we prioritize the accountability of BIPOC states over predominantly white states because of their influence within the international community?

FRENCH: White supremacy, right. Jessica, go right ahead.

WOLFENDALE: I think there are kind of two separate questions in your question, actually, so I'm going to talk a little about the first part: about the influence of white supremacy and lack of accountability, and again, specifically, mainly in the American context. So if you come tomorrow, *[laughter]* I will talk more about this, but I think if you look historically, specifically, I was focusing primarily on torture, but what I say would expand to other atrocities committed against BIPOC people historically, starting with colonization, when torture was used by white colonists and militia against indigenous peoples, but not against fellow white colonists.

You know, all the way through the institution of slavery, and then torture in the Philippines against Filipinos, and then you could talk about public lynching—it's a long, long, history of torture of people of color, indigenous people that's been tolerated within America but also forgotten. And I think that forgetting is an important part of maintaining white supremacy because the forgetting of it allows the illusion of American, sort of white moral citizenship as being essentially good and virtuous. So I think this long history of the use of torture and other forms of violence against BIPOC people is a way of both enforcing sort of white moral citizenship by very literally dehumanizing people who are non-white, but then the forgetting of that—the public and political forgetting of that is also an essential part in maintaining the illusion of white virtuous moral citizenship. So that's my take on the white supremacy and the lack of accountability for atrocities, but, in relation to the ICC cases, I will defer to my colleagues.

FRENCH: Did you want to comment on that at all, Silvia?

FERNÁNDEZ: I'm sorry but I don't, I didn't get that part of the question.

FRENCH: I think she was asking primarily whether there are issues around making sure that the victims, when the victims are in this category, that we are calling BIPOC, but the perpetrators are white, are there more complexities either politically or practically in making sure that justice is served?

WOLFENDALE: Basically, are those cases less likely to be prosecuted?

FERNÁNDEZ: Frankly, I don't think so. I think our cases are complex enough. But I don't think this adds, necessarily, a component to that, not at the court. And I would say, and I would like to use this opportunity, also, to talk very much about how much victim-centered the ICC is. The victims have for the first time—now it's being replicated in other systems—but at the ICC victims can have access to justice, they can ask for participation in the proceedings, they can provide information to the prosecutor, and they can participate in the judicial proceedings by giving their views and concerns. This is extremely important also to address these exams, some of the concerns you have expressed. They can participate in the proceedings, not only as witnesses of crimes that they may have seen or suffered, but really to express views and concerns in general. So that will also help the judges to understand the full context of the situation. So victims can participate in all phases, including at the investigative phase, and they can also seek reparations.

FRENCH: Yes, I just wanted to make one practical comment. The rhythm of the university—as some of you may have noticed, some people have moved on. We have just had a changeover to another class period, so some of the students in the audience have had to scurry off to their classes. They were not losing interest; they just want to pass. Yeah, they were not offended, they just want to pass their classes. Back to you, Jessica.

WOLFENDALE: I think in the ICC too if a state is not signed onto the ICC then it can't be subject to prosecution. So, for example, because America is not a member of the ICC, it also isn't going to affect them. The kinds of perpetrators who are able to be held accountable—

FERNÁNDEZ: Oh well, yeah, but that would not be because of the victims in particular—

WOLFENDALE: No, that's right, that's right.

SCHARF: Let me add one other thing. So if you looked at the first fifteen years of the ICC, every single situation before the ICC was an African situation and you could have said, "Well look, this is a bunch of white judges judging African people of black skin in their courtroom," and that looks really bad. But what we see today as the court has grown older and it has expanded its sites, we now have cases before the court pending and percolating up all over the world, so Afghanistan, the Ukraine, Israel, Guatemala, the Philippines. It's not just Africa anymore.

FRENCH: And the judges themselves are diverse.

FERNÁNDEZI: Well exactly, I wanted to say that. The judges aren't all white.

SCHARF: They are, they are. They are diverse. That's right.

FRENCH: Or all male!

FERNÁNDEZI: Or all male.

SCHARF: And in fact that's by the statute. There are actual distribution requirements.

FERNÁNDEZ: Indeed it is multicultural, and that is represented in the judiciary.

FRENCH: So no one's going to like to hear this but I think we only can take one more question, the rest of you are going to just throw daggers at me with your eyes! That would be you, sir.

AHMED ALAIAT: I promise it will be so quick. I am Ahmed Alaiat. I am a student at Case Western Reserve. My question is exactly about Libya, and we had two different incidents in 2011, when Libya was referred by the US council to the ICC, and the ICC requested surrounding some individuals, including Saif al-Islam, to the court. We have different incidents in 2019, sorry, which is when the "so-called" the commander Haftar launched an attack on Tripoli killed and dislocated many, many Libyans, and the impact is gonna be for a long [time]. So these two incidents and the first occasion, Libya is not a part of ICC, but ICC requested surrounding this individual, based on the referral from—

FRENCH: From the referral from the security council.

ALAIAT: Security council. And in the other incident no one talked about surrounding after or the demand to surrender him. So this is, the question and, I mean, whether we are facing, you know, a double standard or are we in a drop off of the ICC, despite the optimism that you mentioned? But I shared with you this question.

SCHARF: So when the security council referred the matter, it wasn't a referral of individuals. It was a referral of a situation, and it was open-ended. It was basically any war crimes, crimes against humanity that resulted from the Arab Spring conflict, which I would argue is still going on in Libya and therefore the jurisdiction still pertains, even to the incident of 2019 which could ultimately be investigated and prosecuted by the ICC without a new referral. Does that make sense?

FERNÁNDEZ: It makes a lot of sense, but it is something that would need to be looked at by the prosecutor of the ICC in the first place and then the judges. But yeah, that would be my understanding would be around this. But I would like to go back to what you have said, Michael. The issue is always about cooperation, and even when there have been referrals by the security council, there has been problems of when you, at the time of arresting individuals and making this more effective, then cooperation was not forthcoming. But in terms of the law, I think the situation may be clearer, yes.

FRENCH: Well, I thank you all for a wonderful discussion, and I am sorry that we couldn't get to everyone's questions. But back on that point of optimism, I am given hope by the fact that there is so much engagement around these vital issues and people wanting to be part of this conversation moving forward. Can you all join me in thanking our incredible panel one more time! On behalf of President Kaler and Provost Vinson, I would like to thank you all here and online for joining us to attend today's Inamori Ethics Prize Academic Symposium as part of the Cox conference as well. We look forward to seeing you next year for the Inamori Ethics Prize events again. And I hope many of you will also join us tomorrow for the second day of the Cox Conference. Thank you again, and have a great rest of your day.

The Power of Real Empathy in Leadership Is Not "Being Nice"

Jacqueline Acho

Do you struggle to engage your employees as a leader or to find inspiration at work under a bad leader? Perhaps you have heard the recent buzz about "empathy at work," but what does that really mean? How can this soft skill have any real impact? I can relate to these questions.

Empathy was not my professional starting point. I earned my doctorate in chemistry at MIT in 1994 and was elected a partner of McKinsey and Company in 2000. I was energized by some of the best science in the world and had many wonderful C-suite, Fortune 500 clients through the years. All of that was nourishing and enriching. Although empathy was important for teaching and client service, those are not the experiences which helped me remember and develop the superpower of empathy as an adult. I profoundly relearned empathy when I became a parent—one of the many opportunities to lean into learning about life beyond work. It turns out one of the best ways to grow empathy is to live a whole life.

Of course, you do not have to become a parent to be empathetic, but there are two times during which our neural networks are especially wired for developing empathy: during early childhood and when parenting very young children. It makes sense that empathy is the tool we need the most when we do not have words—when we, ourselves, are preverbal or are trying to understand if a baby is hot, cold, hungry, or wet when he cannot speak to us.[1] This central and foundational empathy is often referred to as *emotional* or *affective empathy*. It is the most ancient form of empathy, which we share with other mammals like chimpanzees, bonobos, and elephants.[2] The second part of empathy to develop is called *cognitive* or *imaginative empathy*.[3] Cognitive empathy is the form we use when we are trying to mentally put ourselves in someone else's shoes. It is important that our cognitive and affective empathy are in communication, but our education, work, and society often put them at odds. That is part of why growing in leadership is all too often an empathy-sapping experience.

Climbing the leadership ladder typically means sacrificing the time and experiences outside of work that grow both parts of empathy. How many CEOs do you know who were able to be engaged parents or caregivers for elderly parents, much less take care of themselves in a way that promoted and modeled good mental and physical health? Our systems do not support that kind of development in workers, much less leaders. The US ranks last in the developed world for paid parental leave.[4] Last. The US also ranks near the bottom for work-family balance across the globe.[5] Rising in leadership can be a lonely experience—a product of fierce competition and long hours on the job, not so much in relationship with others but ever more isolating. Once at the top, we further separate leaders by expecting them to be all-knowing, superhuman mind-readers. Fearing the consequences of delivering bad news, we resist telling bosses the truth, handicapping their ability to lead. Furthermore, leaders often have to tell themselves stories that justify shutting down affective empathy and conscience in the face of dehumanizing actions (e.g., excessive cost-cutting, overworking employees, topgrading employees), saying it is "good for business" or at least "looks good in the short term," during which most CEOs are evaluated. So, the organizational hierarchies we build end up being pointy pyramids that make uncomfortable seats for leaders, triggering self-preservation rather than grace, generosity, humanity, and empathic development.

So how can we retain empathy and even develop it as a superpower as we grow in leadership? These are questions I started probing more seriously when I started my own strategy, leadership, and cultural transformation consulting firm. Can you fake it till you make it? Does the style from the top trickle down? If someone does not have empathy, can you "train" it into them?

Retaining and growing empathy as we grow in leadership requires a wholesale rethinking of leadership and leadership development. So many of our business practices dehumanize us and the people we serve, whether they are employees or customers. The rationale is that being dispassionate is good for business and necessary for profit. But is it really? How is it going? Are we achieving our ultimate goals?

Are we as innovative as we want to be? A common measure of innovation—total factor productivity—has been growing at a snail's pace, especially when compared to the glory years of the 1950s, so people wonder if we are out of big ideas.[6] Innovation is also an overused word; not all of it is even good. Great innovation is not formulating the next snack chip laced with sugar and MSG that makes us sick and addicted—no matter how much revenues grow. Great innovation is also not repurposing old drugs to medicate our children so that they can sit still during standardized school testing rather than learn in their own styles, at their own pace, inspired from the inside-out. How about the robots that will keep us company in the Alzheimer's unit one day, while our loved ones are busy elsewhere? Maybe they will be on vacation in space by then, since we are making terrific progress on commuter spacecraft—while one in five children in the US is hungry. If we honestly examine our innovations, we have to admit we are not the leaders we hope to be.

How is it going with true diversity and inclusion? Not so well either. Leadership is still dominated by white men, despite all of the hard work of the feminist revolution and civil rights. The leadership pipeline remains leaky for women.[7] Even the NFL had only three Black coaches in 2020, while 70% of the players were African American.[8]

I have found that empathy is the missing link to the innovation and true inclusion we seek, and we have underinvested in this valuable currency for too long. We have not accounted for the externalities of our lack of empathy for future generations and the planet in our accounting books either.

My experience would suggest we can do three things to help leaders grow with empathy: (1) change the way we develop leaders; (2) change the way we practice work and life integration (beyond old notions of "balance"); and (3) invest time and effort, not even so much money, in developing an organizational, cultural currency of empathy. I have done all of this work with clients in the last decade, whether with for-profit companies, a world-class orchestra, a top-notch university, or the Cleveland police. In all of these cases, payoff has been in the end goals that matter most to each organization, such as with the police, where our work drove a 29% decrease in use-of-force, a 45% decrease in citizen complaints, and more than half of the transfers within the department into the district where we started the work. Growing the "soft skill" of empathy has tangible, real-world impact. If the police can grow in empathy, you can too. It shouldn't be so surprising that aligning organizations with what people need energizes them to do the work they are there to do. Most of these changes do not cost a lot. Some cost nothing. It's about looking at work and doing it differently—treating people like people again.

1. **We need to change the way we do leadership development,** making a topic which is usually subjective and mysterious, objective and clear, and anchoring rewards (and punishments) in behaviors that exhibit empathy and humanity (or lack thereof).

FRENCH: Yes, I just wanted to make one practical comment. The rhythm of the university—as some of you may have noticed, some people have moved on. We have just had a changeover to another class period, so some of the students in the audience have had to scurry off to their classes. They were not losing interest; they just want to pass. Yeah, they were not offended, they just want to pass their classes. Back to you, Jessica.

WOLFENDALE: I think in the ICC too if a state is not signed onto the ICC then it can't be subject to prosecution. So, for example, because America is not a member of the ICC, it also isn't going to affect them. The kinds of perpetrators who are able to be held accountable—

FERNÁNDEZ: Oh well, yeah, but that would not be because of the victims in particular—

WOLFENDALE: No, that's right, that's right.

SCHARF: Let me add one other thing. So if you looked at the first fifteen years of the ICC, every single situation before the ICC was an African situation and you could have said, "Well look, this is a bunch of white judges judging African people of black skin in their courtroom," and that looks really bad. But what we see today as the court has grown older and it has expanded its sites, we now have cases before the court pending and percolating up all over the world, so Afghanistan, the Ukraine, Israel, Guatemala, the Philippines. It's not just Africa anymore.

FRENCH: And the judges themselves are diverse.

FERNÁNDEZI: Well exactly, I wanted to say that. The judges aren't all white.

SCHARF: They are, they are. They are diverse. That's right.

FRENCH: Or all male!

FERNÁNDEZI: Or all male.

SCHARF: And in fact that's by the statute. There are actual distribution requirements.

FERNÁNDEZ: Indeed it is multicultural, and that is represented in the judiciary.

FRENCH: So no one's going to like to hear this but I think we only can take one more question, the rest of you are going to just throw daggers at me with your eyes! That would be you, sir.

AHMED ALAIAT: I promise it will be so quick. I am Ahmed Alaiat. I am a student at Case Western Reserve. My question is exactly about Libya, and we had two different incidents in 2011, when Libya was referred by the US council to the ICC, and the ICC requested surrounding some individuals, including Saif al-Islam, to the court. We have different incidents in 2019, sorry, which is when the "so-called" the commander Haftar launched an attack on Tripoli killed and dislocated many, many Libyans, and the impact is gonna be for a long [time]. So these two incidents and the first occasion, Libya is not a part of ICC, but ICC requested surrounding this individual, based on the referral from—

FRENCH: From the referral from the security council.

ALAIAT: Security council. And in the other incident no one talked about surrounding after or the demand to surrender him. So this is, the question and, I mean, whether we are facing, you know, a double standard or are we in a drop off of the ICC, despite the optimism that you mentioned? But I shared with you this question.

SCHARF: So when the security council referred the matter, it wasn't a referral of individuals. It was a referral of a situation, and it was open-ended. It was basically any war crimes, crimes against humanity that resulted from the Arab Spring conflict, which I would argue is still going on in Libya and therefore the jurisdiction still pertains, even to the incident of 2019 which could ultimately be investigated and prosecuted by the ICC without a new referral. Does that make sense?

FERNÁNDEZ: It makes a lot of sense, but it is something that would need to be looked at by the prosecutor of the ICC in the first place and then the judges. But yeah, that would be my understanding would be around this. But I would like to go back to what you have said, Michael. The issue is always about cooperation, and even when there have been referrals by the security council, there has been problems of when you, at the time of arresting individuals and making this more effective, then cooperation was not forthcoming. But in terms of the law, I think the situation may be clearer, yes.

FRENCH: Well, I thank you all for a wonderful discussion, and I am sorry that we couldn't get to everyone's questions. But back on that point of optimism, I am given hope by the fact that there is so much engagement around these vital issues and people wanting to be part of this conversation

In my experience, most organizations get it wrong. McKinsey & Company, one of the top sources of Fortune 500 CEOs, had a disciplined approach which turned reviews into a simple process for anyone, empathetic or not. We adapted this five-part leadership model to the Cleveland police, focusing on the areas that matter most and centering them in empathy: community leadership (because service is the ultimate goal), people leadership (because, like most, the job is ultimately an apprenticeship), vision for policing of the future (since the field needs reimagining), entrepreneurial leadership (the courage to change, even in a top-down paramilitary organization), and administrative leadership (because turning a huge ship requires knowing how to steer it). We clearly defined what unacceptable, good, better, and best looked like in each category and anchored best behaviors in empathy.

We started small, testing the model in new positions such as on our innovation teams. Unqualified success there made it natural to roll out the model to the rest of the Cleveland Police Department. Hiring, firing, promoting, and celebrating people with a clear, logical model anchored in empathy does many important things. It gives people goals and security in their professional development and leaves no room for zero empathy, psychopathic behaviors throughout the department and out in the community.

2. **We need to change the way we integrate work and life.** One positive outcome of the COVID pandemic is a realization that our work and personal lives are not really two separate existences. They never have been, even as we pretended it was so. We are the same people—fathers, mothers, daughters, sons, friends... with caregiving responsibilities and personal needs—at home and at work. No matter how we try to fit into the norms established by a relatively few, largely privileged white men at the top (forever), our gender, race, economic backgrounds, and sexual orientations are what they are. Trying to leave our identities behind was always problematic, resulting in a handful of people with limited experiences deciding what was best for all of us, causing us to check out of work emotionally if not physically. How do we know? Globally 80% of employees are disengaged

at work—disengaged in most of our waking hours! This result is both bad for business and very sad for us personally.

A good starting point is to admit that we waste each other's time far too often and can trust each other to manage our own time much better. Trust is built not by proximity but by honest, empathetic conversations, and shared experiences. The four-day workweek is gaining momentum across the globe,[9] with good reason. Technology has made working remotely entirely possible, and many of us learned some new things about blending home and work during the COVID pandemic, so long as we use technology to save time rather than letting technology use us up. It is not always easy, especially for people with caregiving responsibilities at home (e.g., parents of young children doing remote school and/or who have special needs), but saving time on commutes, unnecessary meetings, and busy work opens up time to do what is needed at home. Cooking meals. Eating together. Offering a safe, empathetic presence. Fitting in meditation. Getting some exercise. Sleeping adequately. Empathy is selfish first and starts at home.

Taking good care is also good for business. Showing up on a Zoom call with a clear agenda and goals and time for each person to be heard feels much more productive if you are not distracted by poor health and/or worried about your home and the people in it. So much of this is obvious. How did we forget? As we come back to work and spend more time together in offices, may we keep the best of the lessons we learned throughout the pandemic. Even without a pandemic, we are all in this together.

3. **We need to invest time and effort—orienting our cultures and organizational practices—to steward a currency of empathy.** We have overcomplicated organizational/cultural development, forgetting what we need most is to treat people like people instead of cogs in a machine. So many of our business practices dehumanize us, which may make people more productive for a short time, but is unsustainable and hurts our trust, our ability to listen to others who are different from us, and the chance we will do anything special together, such as achieve organic innovation.

It is simple really. People need three things to feel good about their work:

a. **Meaning.** Meaning comes from doing something together that is bigger than we can do alone. Yes, we work to make a living, but how much more inspiring it is to somehow, someway, make the world a better place for even one customer, one client, or one coworker?

b. **Personal Growth.** We evolve and grow, or we stagnate and die, including emotionally. When work is a consistent source of learning, supported challenges, and opportunities, it is a far more engaging endeavor.

c. **The chance to bring our wholes selves to work.** Bringing our whole selves to work has a lot to do with flexibility, physically and emotionally. Organizations that allow employees to flex time, as appropriate for their jobs, and value the perspectives they bring from the various facets of life outside of work, win loyalty, engagement, and a shot at true diversity, inclusion, and innovation that reflects *all* constituents.

Meeting our fundamental needs often requires rethinking our business practices, dropping the ones that are not serving human beings anymore, even if your Harvard MBA endorsed them. Competing employees. Fearsome leadership. Cutting costs to the bone and making the employees left behind work crazy hours to meet production goals. Making decisions that save money now or push addictive and unhealthy products (do we really need Jacked Doritos?), destroy the environment, and bankrupt future generations. These tactics may have worked in the short-term to briefly inflate share prices or make legends out of "tough" CEOs (remember "Chainsaw" Al Dunlop?), but do any of us really see them as courageous or brilliant anymore? Not by a long shot. Hindsight is clear. Investing in organizational meaning, personal growth, and letting employees bring their whole selves to work is what we need. It is simple, even if it is not always easy to change.

Leading with empathy is not about being nice, but rather getting these fundamentals right for the people whose work lives you have a responsibility and privilege to steward.

Back to some of the earlier questions. Can you fake it till you make it? In my experience, it is better than not trying and can create some momentum.

Does the leadership style from the top trickle down? Absolutely. Empathy really is a currency that flows. The more you give, the more you get, and it intuitively feels good, so empathy is self-reinforcing. Empathy is not just about shared pain, but also joy and every other emotion. Stifling humanity by leading with fear is a sure killer for organizational empathy and humanity. If someone does not have empathy, can you "train" it into her? This question is tricky. There are certainly people making lots of money promising "empathy training," but what can be learned in a day or a week? Usually, it is cognitive empathy or perspective taking. Without the appropriate changes to make space for affective empathy development, this lopsided empathy development is too often used for persuading, or worse, manipulating customers and/or employees. Do you know who has outstanding cognitive empathy but zero affective empathy according to the Diagnostic and Statistical Manual of Mental Disorders (DSM-5)? Psychopaths.

The ripple effects of empathy—or lack thereof—connect many dots we have been trying to address separately, such as the number of women and African Americans in leadership positions, stagnant innovation statistics that would flourish if teams would really trust each other, and even some of the broader societal challenges like the political divisions we have sown in the last several years. We do not have to agree with each other to empathize, but by empathizing we are likely to find we have more in common than we thought. Empathy starts with recognizing our own triggers, overcoming them, and being able to listen to others, especially those who are different from us. Empathizing with future generations would orient our businesses to produce products that are better for our bodies and the planet. That would be progress. Our children would be less justifiably worried about their future.

These are big dreams. Is empathy really this powerful? It kept you alive when you were a baby. It's been a big part of how humanity has progressed collectively throughout the millennia. We have tried so many ways to fix all of our seemingly disparate modern problems. Yet, so many persist. What have we got to lose by giving empathy its due? Wherever and whenever we organize ourselves into hierarchies, whatever is at the top flows down, including empathy and humanity.

Great leaders have a vital role to play, and empathy can be their superpower.

Notes

1. James K. Rilling and Larry J. Young, "The biology of mammalian parenting and its effect on offspring social development," *Science* 345, no. 6198 (2014): 771–776.
2. Frans de Waal, *The Age of Empathy: Nature's Lessons for a Kinder Society* (New York: Broadway Books, 2010), 68.
3. For a full explanation of the state of science and the empathy circuit, check out Simon Baron-Cohen, *The Science of Evil: On Empathy and the Origins of Cruelty* (New York: Basic Books, 2012), 17–43.
4. OECD Family Database, http://www.oecd.org/els/family/database.htm.
5. OECD Better Life Index, 2017, http://www.oecdbetterlifeindex.org/topics/work-life-balance/.
6. M. C. K., "Was That It?" *The Economist*, September 8, 2012.
7. "Women in Management: Quick Take," March 1, 2022, https://www.catalyst.org/research/women-in-management/.
8. Dawn Westmoreland, "Why Aren't There More People of Color in Leadership Roles?," https://medium.com/equality-includes-you/why-arent-there-more-people-of-color-in-leadership-roles-fdc4ef989668.
9. Jack Kelly, "The Four-Day Work Week is Gaining Big Momentum," Forbes, https://www.forbes.com/sites/jackkelly/2022/02/03/the-four-day-workweek-is-gaining-big-momentum-signing-up-50-organizations/?sh=75f1ee5f67b6.

Unconscious Unethical Pro-Organizational Behavior

Damon Linder and Perry Haan

Introduction

Transformational leadership emphasizes passionate, dynamic, and inspiring communication by a leader with followers (Bass 1990). Further, transformational leadership is associated with leaders broadening and elevating the interests of their followers. In doing so, transformational leaders generate awareness and acceptance of group goals and activities causing followers to look beyond their own self-interest and apply focus on the good/performance of the group or organization.

Charismatic leadership is one of three espoused originally by Weber (1947). Charismatic leadership is based upon the individual displaying exceptional heroism, holiness, or representative character to influence followers. Transformational leadership places more focus on a compelling message that a leader communicates to followers. Charismatic and transformational leadership theories both focus on the leader's ability to inspire followers, often in the same way (McCoy 2020). Accordingly, charismatic and transformational leadership behaviors are often considered to be virtuous, and it is broadly theorized that transformational and charismatic leadership behaviors help avoid organizational ethical failures because of the actions and practices of the leaders (Bass & Steidlmeier 1999; Flanigan 2013).

Burns (1978) stated that authentic transformational leadership can only be undertaken on a moral foundation. Accordingly, any activity not based on this moral foundation should be considered pseudo-transformational leadership (Sartre 1992 as cited in Bass & Steidlmeier 1999). The charismatic/transformational leader, because of the characteristics associated with these types of leadership, may inspire followers to act towards the benefit of the organization. However, the actions undertaken by followers in this context may ultimately be ethical or unethical.

The overarching belief among organizational researchers and leaders is that this unethical behavior is driven by self-interest. This has led to numerous leadership failures within organizations such as Enron, Global Crossings, Lehman Brothers, WorldCom, and Volkswagen. Unethical behavior has been a contributor in each of these cases and, as a result, organizational leadership ethics has been a topic of continued interest to both the general public and researchers alike for many years (Bryant & Merritt 2019).

Unethical pro-organizational behavior (UPB) can be described as acts that are unethical but motivated by a desire to provide a benefit to one's organization and its members (Bryant & Merritt 2019). Whether follower behavior manifests in organizations as UPB may be more related to the follower than the leader. Accordingly, follower-centered research may yield more insight into UPB than a leader-centered research approach.

Focus has been placed on the role that followers play in the occurrence of UPB associated with transformational and charismatic leadership. One observation that has been studied is that, in organizations that have transformational and charismatic leaders, follower UPB is increasing and being encouraged (McCoy 2020). Accordingly, focusing solely on leadership styles and leader actions may not be sufficient for assuring that an organization and its leaders are encouraging and developing an ethical workplace environment. Accordingly, developing an understanding of why followers engage in UPB is important because unethical behavior of followers and the overall negative effects of UPB on individuals and organizations should be reduced.

Follower UPB has negative effects on organizational performance (Effelsberg & Solga 2015; Effelsberg, Solga & Jochen 2014; McCoy 2020). Further, followers will support leaders and engage in UPB even when it is known that the leader has committed unethical actions (Fehr et al., 2020). Specific attributes that may influence follower propensity towards engaging in UPB have been identified (McCoy 2020). Additionally, whether the behavior is intentional or unintentional has been explored (Wang et al., 2021). However, what has not yet been examined is if this behavior is consciously or unconsciously occurring in followers. If follower UPB is being performed unconsciously, new methods of behavior identification and response, perhaps in the form of training, may have to be developed by organizations if UPB is to be reduced.

Literature Review

Unethical behavior has been observed in organizations at the same time that transformational and charismatic leadership practices were found in organizations (McCoy 2020). However, transformational and charismatic leaders are not necessarily knowingly inspiring UPB (Xue et al. 2020). Regardless, the negative effects of such behavior have been documented extensively and include mental effects on individual follower well-being and future careers as well as organizational survival.

Effelsberg et al. (2014) identified a positive correlation between transformational leadership and UPB. Accordingly, new lines of research have been identified that demonstrate that there are potentially negative, unethical contributions to organizations knowingly and unknowingly by leaders who practice transformational and/or charismatic leadership (Zhang et al. 2020).

Charismatic/transformational leaders, because of the characteristics associated with these types of leadership, may inspire followers to act towards the benefit of the organization. However, actions taken by the leader are simply actions. Consideration as to whether the leader or the follower has a greater impact on unethical behavior should be made, as there is still the question of the reasoning behind why some employees perform acts of UPB in response to their leaders, while others do not. Fehr et al. (2020) suggested that employees with high moral disengagement (MD) retain their trust in leaders who act unethically. As a result of this trust in their leaders who act unethically, they derive a sense of having similar values to the leader, which may influence why they choose to follow this leader.

Song et al. (2021) expanded the Fehr et al. (2020) work regarding moral disengagement related to the propensity of followers' UPB. Followers in the presence of leader-follower congruence in MD propensity were more likely to engage in UPB. Also, followers engaged in UPB more when their MD propensity exceeded their leaders' MD propensity, as opposed to when their leaders' MD propensity exceeded their own. Newman et al. (2020) also investigated MD in the workplace. Results showed that MD exerts a significant influence on the work attitudes and behavior of employees at the individual level of analysis.

McCoy (2020) investigated demographic factors associated with follower UPB resulting from their commitment and allegiance to the leader. These specific follower demographics included gender, job tenure, income level, and age. The study found a relationship between transformational leadership and UPB based upon the variables studied which included follower gender, follower job tenure,; follower income level; and follower age. This demonstrated that transformational leadership methods do influence UPB in followers.

Mishra et al. (2021), classified previous studies regarding UPB based on their underlying theoretical perspectives to better understand how UPB unfolds in the workplace. This included the investigation of a possible relationship between UPB and organizational citizenship behavior (OCB). OCB refers to "individual behavior that is discretionary, not directly or explicitly recognized by the formal reward system, and that in the aggregate promotes the effective functioning of the organization" (Organ 1988, p. 4 as cited in Mishra et. al). OCB and UPB are both voluntary and discretionary behaviors performed by followers. Further, while both OCB and UPB perpetuated by followers sought to increase organizational performance, there may be a simultaneous element of self-interest included with these behaviors in followers.

Voluntary behaviors motivated by follower self-interest are not the only factors that should be considered when identifying the propensity of followers to engage in UPB (Wang et al., 2021). Much research has been based on the premise that UPB is performed by followers in an intentional, active, and voluntary manner in response to particular leadership styles. However, there are seemingly required or forced instances of UPB as well. Organizational situations including ethical climate, performance pressure, the threat of job loss, etc. may impact the occurrence of UPB in followers. UPB focusing on extreme voluntary cases are not reflective of the most common form of UPB. Wang et al. (2021) encouraged researchers to consider both voluntary and involuntary UPB to better understand the phenomenon. Voluntary UPB actions are consciously aimed at benefiting the organization. Involuntary UPB actions may go against the follower's beliefs; however, they feel compelled to act.

There is another factor that should be considered when attempting to better understand follower UPB whether the behavior is consciously or unconsciously occurring. Regardless of the motivation for or influence of the occurrence of such behavior, or whether it is voluntary or involuntary, if the follower is unaware that they are engaging in such behaviors, response actions may be difficult to identify. This begs the question of whether UPB is unethical if its actions are being performed unconsciously in response to organizational stimuli.

Analysis

Followers are influenced by those for whom they work. This influence has been shown to lead to unethical behavior performed by the follower to benefit the organization, its members, or their leaders (Effelsberg et al. 2014). Various leadership styles have been shown to influence this behavior.

Graham et al. (2015) found a positive relationship between transactional leadership and UPB, and Effelsberg et al. (2014) observed that transformational leaders may unintentionally encourage subordinates to commit higher levels of UPB through heightening their organizational identification.

UPB has been studied from various perspectives, including individual, organizational, psychological, and leadership (Zhang & Xiao 2020). Initially, more focus was placed on the organizational level and the leader role. More recently, research focus has been placed on the follower's role in the performance of UPB. This includes individual factors such as moral disengagement (Fehr et al. 2020) and demographic factors (McCoy 2020). There seems to be an assumption that the behavior is actively and voluntarily being performed by the follower, indicating that the follower is consciously performing acts of UPB. Further, focus is placed on leader influence and follower outcome behaviors. One area that may be missing from consideration is that of unconscious priming. Unconscious priming effects "involve passive activation of internal mental representations that influence judgments and behavior without the person's intention or awareness" (Bargh 2016, 49). This is an important distinction. Priming involves behavior that the individual did not intend to occur, is not aware of, and cannot accurately describe verbally. Based on the work of Effelsberg et al. (2014), it seems that transformational leadership influences followers to engage in UPB. If the follower unknowingly performs the UPB, then the unethical behavior by followers may be considered as a result of the prime (leadership style).

In the financial services industry, researchers evaluated workplace identity as a prime for investment bankers while they were at home on a weekend (Bargh 2016). Some respondents were asked to describe their work environment. Those employees with their work identity primed were more likely to cheat for monetary gain in a self-reported coin-toss task. A random sample from the same set of investment bankers at home, who were not first primed with their workplace identity, did not cheat. This exercise demonstrated unconscious priming of workplace identities on unethical behavior in the financial services industry. Subconscious ethical and unethical priming had similar effects: they activated moral standards and increased categorization more than neutral priming.

Followers often are assigned goals or objectives from leaders. If the follower is aligned with these goals, priming effects on UPB may be stronger (Bargh 2020). However, priming effects require the follower to be unaware of the influence of the primes. Wang et al. (2021) examined both intentional and unintentional UPB and determined that unintentional UPB is both more pervasive and has a greater impact on organizational performance. In this case, the success or performance of the organization may be the prime with the commission of UPB by the follower as the follower perceives that they are working towards the best interests or needs of the organization.

In the financial services industry example, if the employee was not primed, they did not cheat. Welsh and Ordóñez (2014) found subconscious ethical and unethical priming activated moral standards and increased categorization more than neutral priming. Activating moral standards either subconsciously or consciously reduced respondent propensity to behave unethically.

Emphasis has been placed on determining the relationship between leadership styles, leader-follower relationships, follower demographic characteristics and attitudes, and others. It seems that these efforts have been undertaken to better understand the nature of UPB and its influences. There is now evidence that subconscious ethical and unethical priming influences ethical decision-making via the activation of moral standards (Welsh & Ordóñez 2014). This is true even when participants were unmonitored and given high-performance goals.

Recommendations for Future Research

Focus on particular leadership styles and their influence on follower acts of UPB is important; however, the fact that this behavior may be occurring without direct knowledge by the leader or the follower indicates that identifying influencing factors should be accompanied by practical efforts to mitigate such behavior regardless of which leadership style the leader exhibits.

First, there seems to be little consideration of primes relative to the occurrence of UPB in organizations. By applying the study of primes such as leadership style, leader-follower relationship, follower demographic characteristics and attitudes, or others, perhaps a better understanding of whether UPB is being performed by followers consciously or unconsciously could be made. This, in turn, could aid in the development of organizational training programs and materials to discourage the practice.

Second, Qing et al. (2020) recommend that organizations implement ethical leadership development training programs highlighting ethical organizational behavior and the practice of ethical leadership by managers. We agree with the recommendations made by Qing et al. (2020), as doing so could improve awareness in the management group. Such training actions may include developing programs that encourage all members of the organization to focus and reflect on the ethical and moral issues that they face at work and how to best deal with ethical issues without specific emphasis on manager behavior or leadership style.

Third, research identifying specific primes associated with the unconscious commission of UPB by followers may identify reasons for follower acts of UPB. Once this information is presented to followers, research could be undertaken to determine the effect of leadership style on UPB among a controlled group of followers that have been specifically trained to determine if different leadership styles still encourage the commission of acts of UPB among followers if the prime is removed.

References

Bargh, J. A. 2016. "Awareness of the prime versus awareness of its influence: Implications for the real-world scope of unconscious higher mental processes," *Current Opinion in Psychology* 12, 49–52. DOI:/10.1016/j.copsyc.2016.05.006.

Bass, B. M. 1990. "From transactional to transformational leadership: Learning to share the vision." *Organizational Dynamics* 18 (3), 19–31. DOI:10.1016/0090-2616(90)90061-S109.

Bass, B., & Steidlmeier, P. 1999. "Ethics, character, and transformational leadership behavior," *The Leadership Quarterly* 10 (2), 81–217. DOI:10.1016/S1048-9843(99)00016-8.

Burns, J. M. 1978. *Leadership*. New York. Harper & Row.

Effelsberg, D., Solga, M., Jochen, G. 2014. "Transformational leadership and follower's unethical behavior for the benefit of the company: A two-study investigation," *Journal of Business Ethics* 120, 81–93. DOI:10.1007/s10551-013-1644-z.

Fehr, R., Fulmer, A., & Keng-Highberger, F. 2020. "How do employees react to leaders' unethical behavior? The role of moral disengagement," *Personnel Psychology* 73, 73–93. DOI:/10.1111/peps.12366.

Graham, K., Ziegert, J., & Capitano, J. 2015."The effect of leadership style, framing, and promotion regulatory focus on unethical pro-organizational behavior," *Journal of Business Ethics* 126 (3), 423–436.

McCoy, Wayne L. 2020. "Predictors of willingness towards unethical behavior in followers of charismatic/transformational leaders: A quantitative path analysis study," *Dissertation Abstracts International Section A: Humanities and Social Sciences* 82 (4-A). ProQuest Information & Learning; [Dissertation], Database: APA PsycInfo.

Mishra, M., Ghosh, K. & Sharma, D. 2021. "Unethical pro-organizational behavior: A systematic review and future research agenda," *Journal of Business Ethics*, 1–25. DOI:10.1007/s10551-021-04764-w.

Newman, A., Le, H., North-Samardzic, A., & Cohen, M. 2020. "Moral disengagement at work: A review and research agenda," *Journal of Business Ethics* 167, 535–570. DOI:/10.1007/s10551-019-04173-0.

Pinio, A. J., Young, J. M., McCormick Lavery, L. 2010. "The state of ethics in our society: A clear call for action." *International Journal of Disclosure & Governance* 7(3), 172–197. DOI: 10.1057/jdg.2010.11.

Qing, M., Eva, N., Newman, A., Nielsen, I., Herbert, K. 2020. "Ethical leadership and unethical pro-organisational behaviour: The mediating mechanism of reflective moral attentiveness," *Applied Psychology: An International Review* 69 (3), 834–853 DOI: 10.1111/apps.12210.

Song, J., Yang, J. & He, C. 2021. "Leader–follower congruence in MD propensity and UPB: A polynomial regression analysis," *The Journal of Psychology* 155(3), 275–291. DOI:/10.1080/00223980.2021.1880359.

Weber, M. 1947. *Max Weber: The Theory of Social and Economic Organization*. A. M. Henderson and T. Parsons (Trans.), USA: The Free Press/The Falcon's Wing Press.

Welsh, D. T. & Ordóñez, L. T. 2014. "Conscience without cognition: The effects of subconscious priming on ethical behavior," *Academy of Management Journal* 57(3), 723–742. DOI:/10.5465/amj.2011.1009.

Wang, J., Shi, W., Liu, G. Q. & Zhou, L. 2021. "Moving beyond initiative: The reconceptualization and measurement of unethical pro-organizational behavior," *Front. Psychol.* 12. DOI:/10.3389/fpsyg.2021.640107.

Zhang, C. H., & Xiao, X. 2020. "Review of the influencing factors of unethical pro-organizational behavior," *Journal of Human Resource and Sustainability Studies* 8, 35–47. DOI:/10.4236/jhrss.2020.81003.

Zhang, X., Liang, L., Tian, G. & Tian, Y. 2020. "Heroes or villains? The dark side of charismatic leadership and unethical pro-organizational behavior," *International Journal of Environmental Research and Public Health* 17. DOI:/10.3390/ijerph17155546.

What Are They Thinking? Teaching Ethics Using Games

Richard McConnell and Andrew Thueme

> *What is philosophy all about? It is about trying to understand what you already know, but you know it so well that you have become unaware of it.*[1]

> *Ethics is a form of punishment that we have designed to inflict upon those who themselves have done nothing wrong.*[2]

> *Moral dilemmas are that we don't know and disagree over what is the right thing to do when we are trying to do the right thing. In a test of character, by contrast, what is right and wrong seems pretty clear.*[3]

Students discovering their moral philosophy

The study of ethics is complicated by the perception that many see this subset of philosophy as an overly scholarly pursuit with little application in daily life. However, the above quotes describe certain notions regarding ethics that military professionals should contemplate. For example, it has been argued in earlier articles that everyone has a moral philosophy, but not everyone is aware of it without reflection.[4] [5] [6] As the first quote above suggests, many may be only subliminally aware of their own philosophy. Additionally, the second and third quotes show that often ethics instruction is reactive after a scandal, and there is confusion between what is a moral dilemma versus a test of character. These common misunderstandings served as inspiration for a study conducted at the US Army command and General Staff College (CGSC).

In the 2019 academic year, a mixed-methods study was conducted at CGSC to investigate alternative ways to teach ethics using a gaming approach. One of the lessons during the initial few months of CGSC discussed ethical decision-making using a case study approach. It was proposed that a gaming approach might be appropriate for teaching ethics. Games promote interactive play, which could simulate the context where moral dilemmas occur. Such games reinforce what ethics is all about—decision-making given ambiguous situations where actors might compete or cooperate with each other.[7] Therefore, a control group used the case study approach for instruction and was compared to the test group that learned ethics using games. What follows is a description of what we learned from this experiment and how those lessons might be applied to other kinds of instruction. First, it is important to understand some of the literature that served as the foundation for the study before we discuss the study itself.

A brief literature review

Honor Defined

One of the reasons why ethics instruction, especially in the military context, can be complicated is because some terms might be poorly defined. For example, most of the army values are clearly defined, while honor is simply defined as "live up to the Army values," which seems like a circular definition.[8] Army leaders might find a re-examining of this central value as a useful pursuit given the importance we place on honor. One could argue that honor is a unifying value that holds all the other values together. Figure 1 depicts how honor could be viewed in its central role.

Figure 1. The unifying army value: honor

An example on how this model could be applied practically could be described as a protocol for leaders struggling with moral dilemmas. For example, leaders who find themselves in situations where they might be encouraged to compromise their integrity might see that as a dishonorable thing to do. Inversely, if leaders are feeling uneasy about a decision they are about to make, they might find that they are being tempted to compromise their integrity. As indicated by the opening quotes above, sometimes leaders must discover right from wrong through reflection. One way to encourage reflection is by starting with the central role of honor and framing it with specific actions in the other army values. This protocol might be useful in general, whereas other scholars have created more specific models worthy of our consideration.

The Ethical Triangle

At the foundation of ethical decision-making are three main areas of accepted thought regarding how ethical/moral behavior is played out in individuals. In his book *Combating Corruption, Encouraging Ethics*[9]; James Svara described these three main areas as the ethical triangle, which is depicted in figure 2.

The ethical triangle depicts virtue, principles, and consequences as three points of the triangle that people use either exclusively or in combination to make moral choices. If I make choices based on what I believe an honorable person might do, perhaps I am operating in the virtue domain. If I spend time considering what laws and regulations apply to the situation, then perhaps I am in the principles domain. If I am concerned about what does the most good for the most amount of people, perhaps I am operating in the consequences domain.

A key aspect of this model is explained in the text above the triangle. If a person prefers one point of the triangle such as virtue to make moral choices, they should avoid using that one portion of the triangle exclusively. The closer to the center of the triangle people are when they make decisions, the better they are. In other words, if someone uses one point of the ethical triangle to initially assess the situation, they could then use the other two points of the triangle as a step for checking their work, that might yield better choices that are more ethically justifiable. The ethical triangle is relevant to this discussion because it was a key concept taught to both the test and control groups in the ethics class. Therefore, determining how effectively students employed the ethical triangle after either a game or case study approach was an important thing to measure to determine the effectiveness of instruction.

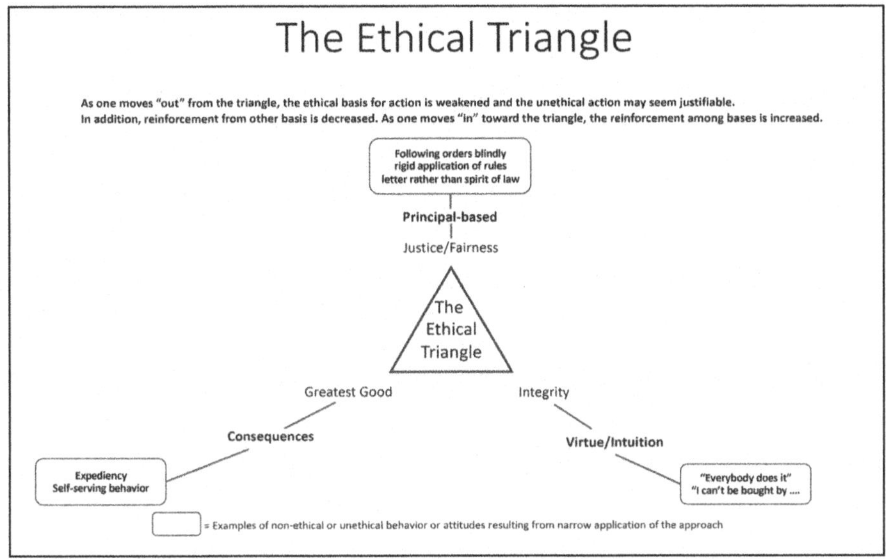

Figure 2. The Ethical Triangle

How we designed the experiment

Before we go into the findings of this study, we first need to explain how the study was set up in greater detail. At CGSC, students are divided into staff groups for their learning based on the adult educational model. The average staff group size is sixteen students. Four staff groups make up one teaching team or student section. All four staff groups share one instructor for their leadership lessons. The study was split between two different student sections. The control group was one section (63 participants) the test group (62 participants) was another section. With a total of 125 participants.

Students in both test and control groups were given a pre-test and post-test. This enabled us to understand where the students were prior to the instruction and examine any differences between the test and the control group post instruction. A mix of quantitative Likert scale questions and qualitative short-answer questions were employed in this mixed-methods study.

Students in the control group received instruction in the normal case study manner. In the test group, students were divided into small teams of four in each staff group. They were given a simple set of instructions to develop solutions to a moral dilemma. Each small team would use their solution to the dilemma as a template to evaluate and assign a score to how their fellow students contended with the dilemma. This approach would essentially enable students to teach themselves the ethical triangle by using it to solve problems and evaluate the moral rigor of other solutions. Student pre-readings for the class remained the same. What is unknown is the level of student's familiarity and experience in studying the ethical triangle prior to CGSC. If you exclusively use army leadership material, it suggests that students had minimal ethical instruction and training prior to the block of instruction given by their CGSC leadership instructors.

What we learned from the experiment

Since this was a mixed-method study, students were given the opportunity to answer questions using a Likert scale for the quantitative data collection and answered open-ended questions for the qualitative data collection. Some statistically significant results were discovered in the quantitative portion of the study (see figure 3) but the most definitive findings came from the qualitative themes collected from both students and from faculty observers (see figures 4 and 5).

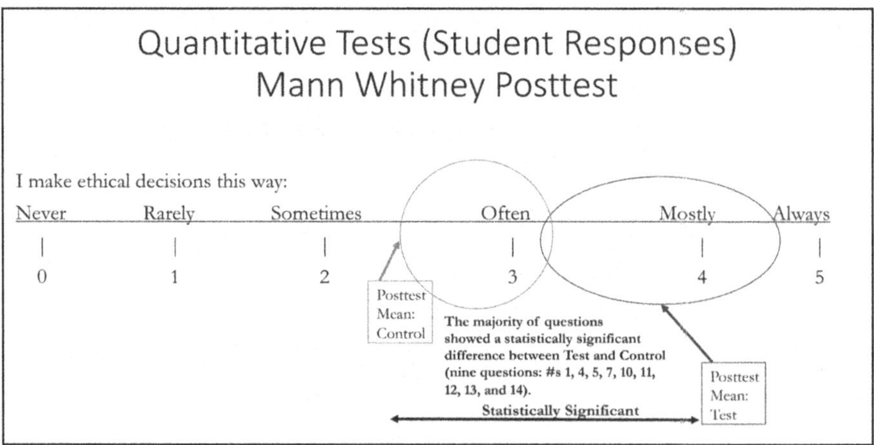

Figure 3. Findings 1

One of the most compelling findings was from a simple question posed to the students, "What aspects of the class should be changed?" We collected an unsolicited response from students responding to this prompt. Three control group students said that they understood the concepts better because of taking the class, compared to ten in the test group. In other words, test group students were over three times more likely to feel that they understood the concepts better having taken the class using a gaming approach.

The above finding generally supported the qualitative results collected from faculty silent observers as well as a four-person faculty focus group

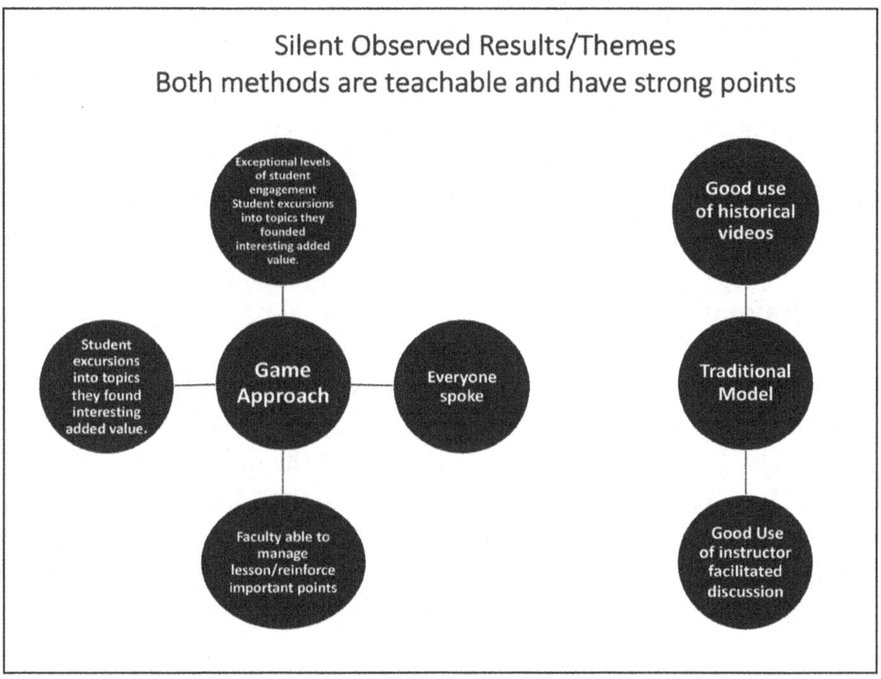

Figure 4. Findings 2

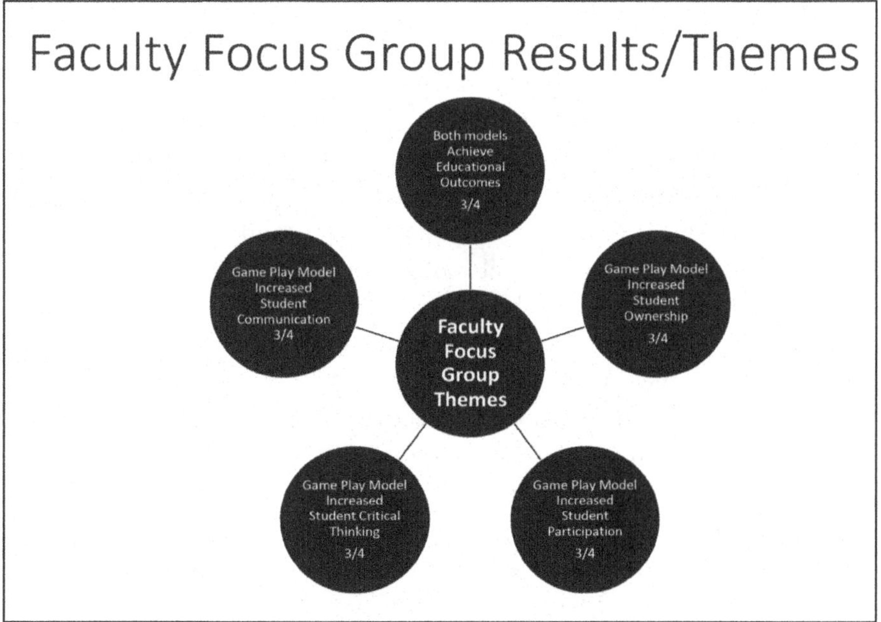

Figure 5. Findings 3

conducted at the end of instruction. In general, faculty observers and focus group members agreed that both methods of instruction were effective but that the gaming approach was by far more engaging. In the ethics game class, students were more likely to be actively involved and learn experientially. Because students had to interact with the ethical concepts and apply them not only to solving a moral dilemma but evaluating somebody else's solution, the concepts were more likely to stick.

Recommendations

The focus of this research has been based on improving ethics instruction using simple gaming. This is built on previous work using gaming to improve visualization within the educational setting. Army leaders may be able to take gaming theory concepts and apply them to ethics training at the unit level and in formal professional military education. Even with the stand up of several institutions for leadership and ethics within the army, most training is still reliant on traditional methods. The use of game theory by army leaders could provide an alternate approach that provides leaders at all levels a chance to discover and reflect.

For example, unit leaders could use the game that this study was based upon (See end notes for link to study research report for detailed game instructions). The ethics game could help leaders at the unit level understand how they make decisions by using the pre-and post-test feedback to understand their ethical preferences. In addition to informing unit leaders to understand their ethical decision-making process, this game could also be used by leaders to help understand where their subordinate element leaders are on the ethical triangle and help them to make sound ethical decisions. This could potentially enable leaders to understand their subordinate's decision-making processes, thereby allowing senior leaders to make better decisions or at least consider how their subordinates make critical decisions. Understanding subordinate moral reasoning allows commanders to understand how they need to communicate their decisions down to their subordinates. Such ethics instruction could enable subordinate leaders to better understand their commander's intent and purpose and why their higher echelon leader made some of the decisions that they did.

This simple game can be run in a matter of minutes without much preparation and does not take up valuable training time. Unit leaders often face challenges in allocating time to training especially in response to ethical and leadership training.

Conclusion

Perhaps it is no great revelation that the experiential approach employed using a game to teach ethical concepts would be more effective. Instruction at CGSC has long emphasized experiential learning at the graduate level. Practical exercises and simulations which encourage higher levels of engagement among students is a time-honored practice in our institution. Employing a simple game clearly raised the level of student engagement. As stated in the introduction, the field of ethics can sometimes be confusing and present challenges in engaging the learning audience. Making the ethics class a game encouraged students to go beyond simple comprehension to successfully manipulate and apply the concepts in real time. Instruction using games is clearly a best practice that should be considered to a greater extent in our professional military education system.

Notes

1. Einar Øverenget, "Why Good People Do Bad Things" (TEDEX, Oslo, Norway, May 17, 2017), https://www.youtube.com/watch?v=AndXsPdvHCM.
2. George Lucas, "Ethical Pluralism in Military Conflicts: Which Side Defends a Just Cause for War?" (Ethics symposium guest speaker, Ethics Symposium, Fort Leavenworth, Kansas, April 30, 2018), 8:40, https://www.youtube.com/watch?v=UX3Vzh4mLxQ.
3. Lucas, 13:00.
4. Richard McConnell and Evan Westgate, "What We Are Thinking: Discovering Your Moral Philosophy Using the Forensic Approach," in *The Impact of Diverse Worldviews on Military Conflict* (2018 annual ethics symposium, Fort Leavenworth, Kansas: CGSC Foundation Press, 2018), 82.
5. Richard McConnell and Evan Westgate, "What Were You Thinking: Discovering Your Moral Philosophy Using the Forensic Approach," *The International Journal of Ethical Leadership* 6, Fall 2019 (October 2019): 70–71.
6. Richard McConnell et al., "The Ethics Game: A Mixed Methods Examination of Learning Outcomes Using Games," in Developments in Business Simulation and Experiential Learning (Association for Business Simulations and Experiential Learning (ABSEL), University of Pittsburgh, Pittsburgh Pennsylvania: ABSEL, 2020), 281.https://absel.org/?page_id=22.
7. Steven Tadelis, *Game Theory: An Introduction*, 1st Edition (Princeton; Oxford: Princeton University Press, 2013).
8. Department of the Army, ADP 6–22: Army Leadership (Washington, DC: US Government Printing Office, 2012), 1–12.
9. James Svara, *Combating Corruption, Encouraging Ethics: A Practical Guide to Management Ethics* (New York: Rowman and Littlefield Publishers Inc., 2011).

A Mosotho Model of Ethical Leadership

Khali Mofuoa

Introduction

> *There are big men, men of intellect, intellectual men, men of talent and men of action; but the great man is difficult to find, and it needs—apart from discernment—a certain greatness to find.*
>
> —*Margot Asquith 2010*

Asquith's statement could not be truer today, as Africa stands reliving its chequered history of leaders from past into present-day Africa. Indeed, African history has had and still has a strange relationship with leaders and leadership. This is the message that one comes across out of the film, *The Last King of Scotland* (2006). For love of the art of cinema, the brilliance of the film induces one to view it, but there is a philosophical side of the film that compels one to see it. That philosophical side of the film leads one deep into the African theatre of sociopolitical milieu that shapes the destiny of leaders and their leadership. It also leads one deep into the heart of the role of the African intelligentsia for engaging African leaders in dialogue on the critical issues of Africa's future. One of the obvious issues for such dialogue compellingly includes the role of ethical leadership–what is the moral responsibility of the African leaders and intelligentsia in contemporary African society?

It is the philosophical side of the film that leads one to go in the annals of African history to uncover, or rather, rediscover Chief Mohlomi, an African Mosotho leader who lived at *Ngoliloe* (where it is written) near the present town of Ficksburg *(Mengeleng)* in the South Africa's Free State province north of Lesotho around 1720–1815 (Mofuoa 2021, 103). This was the place where (1) Mohlomi chieftaincy headquarters were as he presided over his chiefdoms, (2) he established his leadership academy for would-be chiefs, and (3) he died at the age of ninety-six.

Mohlomi is regarded as one of the best examples of the brilliance of ethical and intellectual leadership in precolonial Southern Africa. Commenting on one of the Mohlomi's acclaimed achievements, Machobane (1978, 5) writes,

"Far from being a footnote in his achievements, [Mohlomi] was a political tutor to [Moshoeshoe, a Mosotho leader who founded the Basotho nation around 1824 in present-day Lesotho]. It is Mohlomi who gave [Moshoeshoe] the political alternative of building a nation in Southern Africa, the alternative which thrust him to greatness." Commenting further on Mohlomi's encounter with Moshoeshoe as one of the highlights of his illustrious career, Thompson (1975, 27) notes, "Mohlomi seems to have stimulated Moshoeshoe's ambition and encouraged him to behave humanely and rationally."

Corroborating the same point, Sanders (1975, 22) remarks thus, "Before meeting [with Mohlomi], Moshoeshoe was forceful and domineering, and so determined to assert his authority." However, after meeting Mohlomi, Sanders (1975, 22) states that, "[Moshoeshoe] became a completely changed character [as] he began to be noted for his many acts of kindness and generosity." Sanders (1975, 22) notes that, having grasped Mohlomi's political leadership lessons/methods, Moshoeshoe was determined to follow them. Indeed, according to Sanders, "The debt that [Moshoeshoe] owed to Mohlomi was considerable, and he later freely acknowledged it" (Sanders 1975, 22).

In leadership, Mohlomi's teachings and works remain particularly instructive given his successful application of unorthodox philosophies in illuminating the role of ethical leadership in the management and governance of public affairs (Mofuoa 2021). As such, whatever was the focus of his teachings and works; they are bound to provoke widespread intellectual interest and attention in contemporary Southern Africa. This paper presents Chief Mohlomi as a model of ethical and intellectual leadership enterprise in Southern Africa. It provides an insight into the making of his life, career, and scholarship. It traces the historical factors, experiences, and contours which shaped his personality, worldview, and teachings. It captures the gamut of issues which influenced aspects of his thought and contributions to the enterprise of ethical leadership, of social and of political behavior. All these are done to explain the implications of aspects of his teachings and works for the contemporary Africa's ethical and intellectual leadership development project whose aim is to empower African leaders to deal with critical issues of Africa's future responsibly.

Mohlomi: A Brief Biography and Sociopolitical Appreciation

> *The course of every intellectual, if he pursues his journey long and unflinchingly enough, ends in the obvious, from which the non-intellectuals have never stirred.*
>
> —*Aldous Huxley 2004*

Chief Mohlomi was born around 1720 at *Fothane* near the present-day town of Fouriesburg *(Mashaeng)* in the South Africa's Free State province north of Lesotho (Mofuoa 2021, 130). He was born during the great migration of the Sesotho-speaking people (Basotho) in search for suitable settlement. Struggles for status and power, which resulted in movements of emerging political groupings, characterized the migration period. Mohlomi's clan of *Bakoena* (the crocodile) were not immune from these struggles that led "to quarrels for status marked by violence and splits of [clans/tribes] into sub-chiefdoms, each trying to form an independent dynasty" (Machobane 1978, 8). This history of violent and fragmented political dispersal among *Basotho* tribes was well known to Mohlomi, who was convinced that it was "a needless and self-defeating way of life" (Machobane 1978, 9).

Mohlomi made his mark in his society as a doctor (*Ngaka*) and rainmaker (*Moroka-pula*), (Machobane, 1978: 12). As a *Ngaka* and *Moroka-pula,* he had a very high reputation throughout Southern Africa. He travelled (1) on calls for healing and rain-making services (Mofuoa 2015, 104) and (2) in search of knowledge and remedies (Macgregor, 1905: 13; Mofuoa, 2015:104). As a keen political observer, Mohlomi's medicine and rain-making travels enabled him also to preach peace and resolve conflicts through peaceful means in societies he visited. Arbousset and Daumas (1846, 281) note that in his visits "he would settle the differences of the people when they desired him, and he entered into treaties of alliance with the chiefs recommending them to cultivate peace." As a messenger of peace, he adopted peaceful means of cementing friendship among polities for social and political reasons (Mofuoa 2015, 104). As a rainmaker, he was held in high repute" (Ellenberger and Macgregor, 1912). He was known as "a man of goodwill and humanity" (Macgregor 1905, 13) and "a man of much benevolence" (Machobane 1978,14).

Mohlomi was a celebrated chief and sage (Mofuoa 2021,131). As a chief, it is said that Mohlomi's conduct of the political affairs of the people of *Monaheng* was admirable and exemplary (Machobane 1978, 16), and "his government was that of a prince distinguished for clemency and wisdom" (Arbousset and Daumas 1846, 272–275). As a sage, Mohlomi was considered as "the wisest man that had ever lived" (Machobane 1978, 17). His aphorisms like "medicine for a village is a good heart" and "it is better to grow corn than to brandish the spear," which spelled the themes of peace and justice and showed his sagacious frame of mind on sociopolitical matters.

Mohlomi was also a renowned philosopher of his time (Mofuoa 2021, 131). Unable to accept some of his society's basic assumptions about existence, he is said to have preoccupied his mind with such questions (Machobane 1978 cited in Mofuoa 2021, 131). Arbousset in Ellenberger (1912, 92) notes some of the questions which used to occupy Mohlomi's mind thus, "Where does the world end? Does anything create itself?" With these unusual questions of existence, Mohlomi is credited for playing a special philosophical role in the field of ideas that was outside the scope of Basotho collective wisdom at the time. Whence, Mohlomi was, in a real sense, a philosopher (Machobane 1978, 18).

Mohlomi was also an acclaimed prophet whose prophecies made him a leading figure of his time. From his birth, he is said to have been mystic (Mofuoa 2021,131). Machobane (1978) notes that the first sign of it happened in a dream while at *Mophatong* (initiation school) undergoing initiation. Here, it is said that Mohlomi was told by *Balimo* (ancestors) that, "After some time, you will be a king; you should rule our people well [with peace] and study medicines, so that they may not be trouble by illness while you are still around" (Machobane 1978: 12).

The second happened on the evening of his death. Here, Mohlomi is said to have fallen into a trance and when he woke up, he had a message to tell the waiting mourners, "After my death, a cloud of red dust will come out of the east and consume our tribes" (Ellenberger and Macgregor 1912, 97). Thus, Mohlomi is accredited for predicting *Lifaqane* (wars of calamity) associated with state formation and expansion in Southern Africa in the early 1800s. Such was the end of Mohlomi, "th[e] man who was the most famous of all Basot[ho]—famous for his love of peace, for his charity to all, for his wisdom and for love he bore to all men" (Ellenberger and Macgregor 1912 cited in Mofuoa 2015, 105). In what follows, the paper locates Mohlomi within the sociopolitical problems of his time that honed his theoretical orientation and intellectualism during precolonial Southern Africa.

Mohlomi and the honing of his theoretical orientation and ethical intellectualism

In a poetic summation of the challenge of Africa, Jean-Marc Ela quoted in Matthews (2004, 381–82) writes,

> Africa is not against development. It dreams of other things than the expansion of a culture of death or an alienating modernity that destroys the fundamental values so dear to Africans...Africa sees further than an all-embracing world of world material things and the dictatorship of the here and now that insists on trying

> to persuade us that the only valid motto is "I sell, therefore I am." In a world often devoid of meaning, Africa is a reminder that there are other ways of being.

Indeed, as a film about leadership, *The Last King of Scotland (2006)* is arguably one of the best history lessons about leaders in Africa. It is a tale about leaders' personal moral failings and moral ambivalence that provide flashes of insight into the sociopolitical milieu of African society. It turns into a pointed signal of what happens when intellectuals forget that independent thought that engages in analysis rather than advocacy is the foundation of human progress and development. Undoubtedly, the film speaks to the sociopolitical milieu of Mohlomi's precolonial time that honed his theoretical orientation and intellectualism over time to become a doyen of Southern Africa's sociopolitical and ethical reformer geniuses of all time.

Before the 1800s, Southern Africa's people, including Basotho, were loose communities set within small chiefdoms with no overall ruler (Mothibe 2002 cited in Mofuoa 2016, 165). Although elements of patriarchy and communal ownership were widely practised, most of the customs and traditions were generally in flux (Gill, 1993 cited in Mofuoa 2016, 165). One author has described Basotho traditions as "frequently innovative, localized and contested" (Epprecht, 1992 cited in Mofuoa, 2016:165). This nature of the traditions provides the sociopolitical context of Mohlomi's time and explains the sociopolitical problems of his time that shaped his theoretical orientation and intellectualism in ethical leadership. These sociopolitical problems include but are not limited to abuse of power by chiefs, armed conflict between clans and tribes, abuse of alcohol and dagga, witchcraft, and the weak position of vulnerable people like women and children. In the paragraphs to follow, some of these sociopolitical problems would be spelt out with a view to highlight Mohlomi's moral plight on them and how they shaped his socioethical and political outlook in general.

Abuse of power by chiefs: During the days of Mohlomi, chieftainship was the lifeblood of the social, spiritual, economic, and political being of Southern African societies. Its social, spiritual, economic, and political power and relevance drew from a cultural etiquette that has been hard to shake off. In the formative days of the Basotho nationhood, chieftainship was important as a unifying symbol of society (Juma, 2011, 128). It has significance as the symbol of a nation's cohesion and identity and provided unity in the consciousness of the Basotho. In the chieftainship system, the chief in a sense became the ultimate "ruler, judge, maker and guardian of the law, repository of wealth, dispenser of gifts, leader in war, priest and magician of the power" (Schapera 1938, 62).

In essence, the chief had massive authority and power in the body politic of society. Generally, the economy revolved around the chief and the homestead (Juma 2011, 128). The chief was to be supported by all as his wealth fed the impoverished, supported military expeditions, and ran the administration (Mothibe 2002, 21). Thus, paying tribute in the form of *matsema* (communal labour), suppling animal products and participating in the decision-making process were all an essential part of community life (Gill 1993, 49). The chiefdoms were held together by intricate political, social, and economic relationships galvanized by consultation at multiple levels and consensual support (Gill 1993, 49).

Eventually, the amassing of social, spiritual, economic, and political power by the chiefs led to abuses. Personal overzealousness, authoritarianism, irreplaceability, and infallibility suddenly became the ethos of political leadership of chiefs. Nepotism, corruption, uneven application of the law, arbitrary rule, and a myriad of other abuses of power became the order of communal life in some societies. Mohlomi resented and rejected these abuses of power by chiefs as leaders, which have become a way of life in sub-Saharan Africa today (Nicolaides and Duho 2019; Transparency International 2021). For the entirety of his life, he took upon himself to travel throughout Southern Africa, preaching against the evils of the abuse of power by leaders. No wonder Mohlomi took upon himself to establish his leadership academy at *Ngolile* to educate the would-be leaders (chiefs) on the idea and ideals of ethical leadership (Mofuoa 2014, 86–109) to empower them to deal with critical issues of their society's future including abuse of power that is often coupled with endemic corruption.

Armed conflict between clans and tribes: During Mohlomi's time, the violent scramble for suitable land for settlement was the order of the day (Arbousset and Daumas 1846, 131; Ellenberger and Macgregor 1912, 18–68). In the heart of that scramble was cattle raiding, which was an accepted norm of communal life in Southern Africa at the time. Clans and tribes built their names, influence, and wealth by seizing cattle from their wealthy or weak neighbours. The raids were usually accompanied by bloody massacres and the scattering of survivors. To Mohlomi, cattle-raiding expeditions were nonsensical, as they caused unnecessary armed conflict between clans and tribes resulting in bloodshed and suffering—he would have condemned the remaining deadliest Africa's armed conflicts in Democratic Republic of Congo (DRC), Somalia, South Sudan, Nigeria, Central African Republic (CAR), and Libya. He would have done so because he believed that the practice of peace was the first and foremost prerequisite for good governance. Throughout his entire life, he sought to live in peaceful coexistence with his neighbors and encouraged habits of thrift and industry among his people.

Other than cattle raiding, armed struggles for status and power and the resultant violent emerging political groupings were the features of Mohlomi's time (Machobane 1978, 8). The struggles for status and power, which were interclans and tribes and/or intraclans/tribes, were usually long, theatrical, and disruptive (Machobane 1978, 8). They were accompanied by violent catastrophic wars and battles because of which many people were unnecessarily killed (Damane 1976, 3–4). These violent struggles were sometimes over the status differences between the sons of chiefs and/or the customary arrangement of *Lekenelo*—the right to the widow's hut and responsibility for her necessities (Machobane 1978, 8). As a result, clans and tribes kept intermittently moving and dispersing throughout Southern Africa (Machobane 1978, 8). This history of the violence and fragmentation of his people was known to Mohlomi, and it is evident that Mohlomi hated it (Ellenberger and Macgregor 1912, 13). It is said that Mohlomi had tried to prevail over his people to cease waging wars needlessly. For him, all the fighting was "a needless and self-defeating way of life" (Machobane 1978 cited in Mofuoa 2015, 103). In the main, he believed that "peace, goodwill and humanity" were the better alternative to "the washing of spears" in the neighbours' blood (Ellenberger and Macgregor 1912,13).

Witchcraft: During Mohlomi's time, witchcraft was a common practice in Southern Africa. It was attributed to a strong belief in magic and invisible forces for explanations and reasons for inexplicable life situations. In essence, the belief in magic and mystical powers was thought to be helping people to find explanations when things went wrong. As Mbiti (1991, 168) explains,

> By putting the blame on the practice of magic or sorcery or witchcraft by someone in the community, people are able to reach an answer which appears to them satisfactory. Such an answer harmonizes with the view of the universe which recognizes that there are many invisible forces at work and that some of them are available to human beings.

Mbiti (1991) goes further to emphasize the importance placed on any invisible forces governing the universe in communal life thus: the communities need these beliefs [as] the factor for stabilizing relations among relatives, neighbors, and members of the community. The belief, and sometimes fear, of these magical forces creates a sense of responsibility for each person to uphold their morals and duties within society. It keeps people from offenses like stealing, rudeness, committing crimes, or even deliberately offending someone (Mbiti 1991, 168).

Although African people believe in the positive attributes of mystical forces, they understand that if placed in the wrong hands, these forces can be used in malice to create harm (Okonkwo et al. 2021; Isiko 2019; Mufuzi 2014; Peach 2002; Mbiti,1991; Ray 1976; Nadel 1952; Parrinder 1954). This was the same conviction that Mohlomi had during his time. It is the same conviction that drove Mohlomi to total war with evils of witchcraft, which still bedevil present-day twenty-first-century societies in Africa and in other parts of the world, resulting in the declaration of August 10 as a World Day against Witch Hunts (Müller and Sanderson 2020). In fact, in modern-day African cultures, aspects of witch-magic still occupy center stage in African social life despite their destructive social maladies on the social ordering of communities (Quarmyne 2011, 475–507; Isiko 2019, 83–96; Okonkwo et al. 2021, 446–464).

As a healer, Mohlomi is said to have never thrown *litaola* (the bones) and ridiculed those who worked on the credulity of the people by means of them (Ellenberger and Macgregor 1912, 92). He is also said to have hated "quacks" i.e., those practitioners of his time who specialized in "smelling out" people suspected of witchcraft in society (Machobane 1978, 11–12). To demonstrate his disdain for such practitioners, an instance is recorded at which he conducted an experiment before the public by which he convinced the spectators of the unscientific nature of the practice of "smelling out" and delivered a speech urging his people to avoid the witch doctors whose bad faith he had just exposed (Ellenberger and Macgregor 1912, 92–93). Indeed, during Mohlomi's time, the fake healers who selfishly manipulated magic and mystical powers caused harm to communal life, often resulting in conflict and killings, which Mohlomi preached against. Thus, during Mohlomi's time, violent repression and armed struggles against so-called witchcraft led to a culture of violence in societies where innocent lives were lost needlessly. It regrettable that in modern-day African societies the witchcraft phenomenon is still an integral part of the way of life in African cultures (Mufuzi 2014, 50–71)

Abuse of alcohol and dagga: Like the rest of Africa, Southern African societies were no strangers to the problem of abuse of alcohol and dagga. When Africans first began using cannabis as a drug is not known, but the practice of cannabis was very much alive and widespread throughout Africa (Walton 1963; van der Merve 1975; Walton 1963, 85–113). Thus, by the time of Mohlomi, nearly all Southern Africa's societies had established dagga cultures for social, economic, and religious reasons (Vedder 1966, 175; Junod, 1912, 342–345; Purvis 1909, 336–337). In some tribes like the Zulus and Sothos, warriors also used dagga before going into battle . Speaking of the Sotho, Livingstone (1857, 540) wrote that the warriors "sat down and smoked it [hemp] in order that they might make an effective onslaught."

Whatever the use, dagga was often abused with dire consequences for human dignity. For instance, dagga smoking assumed a special importance in jurisprudence in some tribes whereby anybody accused of a crime was required to smoke dagga until he admitted his crime. More serious crimes were accompanied by additional punishments. It is these kinds of abuses that Mohlomi preached and taught against in Southern Africa societies of his time. He also spoke against the use of alcohol and dagga for health reasons—their short- and long-term effects on people who abuse them, which include brain damage, lung infections, and unhealthy loss of weight. In fact, Mohlomi would be disappointed that abuse of alcohol and dagga is still rife in modern-day societies around the globe (Peltzer and Phaswana-Mafuya 2018, 1–6; Cunningham and Koski-Jännes 2019,1–6).

The weak position of women and children in society

The role of women and children, their position and status in society, and their nature have been issues of debate and discussion informed by religion, tradition, and culture from time immemorial. This was the case in the Southern African society where Mohlomi grew up and lived. The perceptions of women during Mohlomi's time can be summarized thus,

> Women are "inferior" and "unequal" to men. Women are ... weak, inferior, inherently evil (it is the nature of woman to promote mischief) ... have deficient intellectual capabilities and are spiritually lacking. [As such] ... women are unsuitable for performing certain tasks, or for functioning in some ways in society (Peach, 2002).

The view of women as inherently evil explains why the blame for misfortune, death, and illness often fell on women in communities during Mohlomi's time. It seems that the popular opinion saw women generally as witches and evil-doers within communities (Peach 2002, 302). In a similar fashion, Parrinder (1954, 131–124) puts the common view of the practice of witchcraft among women in most African religious tribes thus,

> Women are the most prone to suspicion of witchcraft. In some parts of Africa all witches are believed to be female, and that the mother passes down her witchcraft to her daughter [girl-child].

The view of the role of witchcraft as uniquely possessed by females led to horrendous punishments of the suspected women and girl-child witches by communities, often resulting in the death penalty. For instance, this was among the Cape Nguni and/or the Zulu (Mahao 2010, 332). Accused witches were subjected dreadful techniques to prove their innocence or guilt. Parrinder (1954,127) notes some of the techniques used to force women into submission of witchcraft guilt or innocence thus:

> This may consist of some semi-poisonous matter to be swallowed....The accused witches had to drink a reddish soapy medicine out of bottles....The witches also had to surrender their horn of witchcraft, and if they denied having any their houses would be searched.

It is these very perceptions about women and children, and the girl-child in particular, that Mohlomi preached against. He travelled throughout Southern Africa, impressing on communities the need to be wary of the death penalty in general, and never to impose it for alleged witchcraft, which was often targeted at women and children (girl-children). In one of his lectures to Moshoeshoe, Mohlomi is reported to have said,

> One day you will truly be a chief and ruler over men. Learn to understand men and know their ways. In their disputes, adjudicate with justice, perfect justice, and sympathy. You should never sentence anybody to dearth who is accused of sorcery. Keep a careful watch on doctors—most of them are false healers and shameless liars who instigate endless quarrels and conflict among people (Mokhehle 1976, 31–32).

From the quotation above, there is no doubt that the issue of the weak position of women and children in society was close to Mohlomi. He believed that it was one of the biggest challenges facing the society of his time. Mohlomi would be disappointed about the number of shocking incidents of violence against women and girl-children in modern-day societies. He would agree that gender-based violence is "a public health and human rights issue affecting women and girl-child around the globe" (Kennedy 2017). He would have continued to condemn "violations of [women's and] children's rights that remain tragically common across the world" (Ortiz-Ospina and Roser 2017). He would have also whole-heartedly supported effective and scalable societal efforts to address them (Fry and Elliot 2017). As has been shown herein, Mohlomi's scholarship and career represented a refreshing engagement with the significant sociopolitical problems of his time. Having located him within the sociopolitical milieu of his time during precolonial Southern Africa, which honed his evergreen theoretical orientation and intellectualism, the next section discusses his invaluable contribution to African knowledge production and intellectualism.

Mohlomi's contribution to African knowledge production and ethical intellectualism

In *Powerlessness, Lamentation and Nostalgia: Discourses of the Post-Soviet Intelligentsia in Modern Latvia*, Procevska (2010, 47) writes,

> Distance and strangeness have been viewed as natural characteristics of an intellectual. Intellectuals are said to dwell in the lands of ideals and goals, usually leaving practical matters to others and moving on to new ideals and goals. Thus, an intellectual is never home, never settled down; he is meant to be nomadic because being on a quest is the essence of being an intellectual. Attachment and engagement are viewed as a threat to the freedom of his thought and successful functioning of the intellectual."

These remarks about the nature of intellectuals' rings true of Mohlomi. As Ellenberger (1912, 90) notes, "There was nothing very remarkable in his appearance. He wore *letjekoana* (a collar of brass) round his neck, and large pendent earrings... [yet] Mohlomi was born great, as if he had greatness in respect of chieftainship thrust upon him. It was a distinction for which he cared little, and the great part he played in the history of his country was due rather to his personal attributes than those he acquired by reason of his position in the world. He was no warrior, [and] there are no conquests or extension of power record; but the influence he acquired over his own people and other nations far and near was very great indeed, and on the whole, it was an influence for good." It is Mohlomi's "influence for good" that is at the heart of discussions in this section, which discusses Mohlomi's invaluable contribution to the African context knowledge production and intellectualism never seen or experienced before in Southern Africa at the time.

Art of healing: As a doctor and psychiatrist, Mohlomi's contribution to the art of healing in Southern Africa is well recorded (Guma 1960; Machobane 1978; Mokhehle 1976; Ellenberger and Macgregor 1912). He is said to have created a platform for broad understanding and social appreciation of the art of healing in Southern Africa, particularly in Lesotho. He seemed to have had a rationale behind his cultural and traditional healing practices where, amongst others, he is said to have used herbs and psychological support to achieve optimum results. As Mbiti notes, "[The] medicine-man applies both physical and 'spiritual' or psychological treatment" (Mbiti 1990). His new approach to healing and the methods he applied thus radicalized healing as was known in the social circles at the time. He was regarded as the greatest healer of all time with immense knowledge of healing and understanding of the human condition. He was able to distinguish between real and pretentious doctors whom he advised and preached against. In this regard, there is no doubt that he would have been comfortable with modern healing, as it often entails the very practices that he valued.

Art of travelling: As a prolific and legendary traveller, Mohlomi made an immense contribution to the art of travelling in Southern Africa. In fact, he is said to have introduced a totally new culture of travelling in Southern Africa, particularly among Basotho. In Sesotho, travelling is linked to cultural and empirical knowledge, in ways that transcend and ultimately transform the mundane but encompassing reality of life. As the *maele* (proverbs) puts it: *Ho tseba naha ke ho bata mohlaba*—i.e., "To know the world, one must walk the countryside." Mohlomi was renowned as the legendary traveller of all time. He said have always travelled about seeking new medicines, healing texts, and cures, hence the *Maele: 'Ngaka e shoa e etile'*—i.e., "a doctor dies abroad" (Guma 1967, 82). Indeed, he met his death from the sickness he got while on one of his many travels (Ellenberger and Macgregor 1912). Thus, the popular tradition is that Mohlomi's travelling escapades made him a renowned source of cultural knowledge and a social reformer of note in Southern Africa.

Art of governance and leadership: As a governance and political leadership consultant, Mohlomi had a passionate interest in the problems of government and governance issues of his time (du Preez 2003,16, Machobane 1978,13). The popular tradition tells that he was typically concerned about

Southern Africa's governance problems of abuse of power, hostility and conflicts and human rights abuses of his time. His contribution to the art of governance and leadership was the unusual political philosophy he practised and taught to the aspiring would-be chiefs at his leadership academy in Ngo-liloe (Mofuoa 2015; du Preez 2012, 2004, 2003; Machobane 1978; Bruwer 1956; Ellenberger 1912). The canons of his political philosophy included but were not limited to: (1) a policy of democracy better captured by his famous saying—*"Morena ke morena ka sechaba"* i.e., "a chief is a chief by the grace of his people"; (2) a policy of peace as fundamental to all good and lasting governments; (3) a policy of leading people by gentleness, and (4) a policy of benevolence towards the distressed. His political philosophy thus implied a different philosophy of leadership for Southern Africa formulated by shared authority as leitmotif of popular governance (Mahao 2010, 322). Humility, fairness, and empathy had to be the stock-in-trade qualities of leadership for the management of public affairs.

Art of diplomacy: As a diplomat, Mohlomi was keenly interested in the problems of international relations and travelled for political and diplomatic reasons. During his legendary travels, he settled political differences amongst chiefs and entered treaties of diplomatic alliance with them recommending them to cultivate peace. He practised polygamy and advised chiefs on it as a means for cementing friendship and diplomatic ties among polities (Macho-bane 1978, 13). Mohlomi is also responsible for establishing the concept of diplomatic immunity in Southern Africa (du Preez 2003,16). It is said he first proposed what became a custom that messengers between chiefs should never be attacked and killed "...instead, you have an obligation to give him food and shelter and help him on his way" (du Preez 2003,16). In the years of great conflict that were to follow, this custom was mostly respected even by great warriors such as Shaka and Mzilikazi (du Preez 2003,16).

Art of conflict transformation through peace-making: As pacifist, Mohlomi was an influential Mosotho peacemaker of eighteenth-century Southern Africa. Ellenberger and Macgregor (1912, 93) write, "Mohlomi...was well received everywhere and consulted as a kind of oracle. Disputes were referred to him, which he adjusted with great wisdom. He was a friend to everyone and urged [them] to love peace." Popular tradition says that he did not only preach peace, but he also practised it. It is said that he disbanded his fighting units telling the warriors to grow food and look after women and children rather than make war. Perhaps, his message of peace was best captured in one of his famous sayings that endured: "It is better to thrash the sorghum than to sharpen the spear." Mohlomi is much celebrated to have set the Southern Africa's famous nineteenth-century Mosotho King Moshoeshoe on his path to peace during his rule. His advice to Moshoeshoe was to always "lean uponthe rod of peace" (Mokhehle 1976, 32). He thus popularized the word *khotso* (peace) that it endured to become a word of greetings among the Basotho (Mokhehle 1976, 32).

Art of philosophy: As a wandering philosopher and sage, Mohlomi was a very prominent figure in philosophical and intellectual history in precolonial Southern Africa. Popular tradition tells how he laid down the philosophy of life with truthfulness, justice, peace, love, compassion, equality, tolerance, conciliation, respect, discipline, democracy, neighbourliness, and friendship as its canons adduced from creative mental and physical experience of the Basotho society. Speaking of Mohlomi's philosophical accolades, du Preez (2003,16) notes, "There were few, if any philosophers, in Southern Africa at the time who preached love, tolerance, compassion, women and children rights, peace, democracy and abstinence." In fact, Machobane (1978, 17–18) further notes, "...Mohlomi's inquisitive mind did not end with questions on and solutions to problems of social [and political] order. [He also]...greatly troubled his mind with the subtle and uncommon problems of existence—how did things come into existence." There is no doubt that he had a special role in the field of ideas that was outside the scope of collective wisdom in Southern Africa at the time (Machobane 1978; Gill 1993; du Preez 2003). As Gill (1993, 24, 59) puts it, "from his studies, [Mohlomi] developed a philosophy [of life] which he practiced and passed on to his disciples. His philosophy cannot be found in long manuscripts, but it has been captured in maxims or proverbs which have since been passed down to succeeding generations." In all its cultural, moral, social, religious, political, and economic discourse, Mohlomi's philosophical heritage was fittingly portrayed by his disciple, Moshoeshoe, who remained steadfast to it (du Preez 2003, 16). In fact, Moshoeshoe famously built Basotho nation on the philosophical ideals propounded, canvassed, and popularized by Mohlomi (Mokhehle 1976, xvi–xviii). Mohlomi completely imbued Moshoeshoe with his philosophy, prophesied for him a great future, and started him off on a road from which Moshoeshoe never swerved.

Conclusion

A decade ago, George Ayittey (2012) tearfully lamented the death of ethical and intellectual leadership in post-colonial Africa. His critical assessment is that, unlike Mohlomi, the contemporary African intelligentsia are "afflicted with intellectual astigmatism" (Ayittey 2012), resulting in their inability to engage postcolonial African leaders in dialogue on the critical issues of Africa's future. As a consequence, "the [contemporary] narrative of African development has become one of advocacy rather than analysis" (Ohiorhenuan 2009, 152). These observations are a sober reminder to contemporary African intelligentsia about their role of engaging post-colonial African leaders in analytical dialogue on the critical issues of Africa's future that Mohlomi demonstrated during precolonial Southern Africa. Indeed, Mohlomi is an ethical aide-mémoire to contemporary African intelligentsia that critical and independent thought is the foundation of ethical and intellectual leadership in society.

The paper has shown that Mohlomi is one of the best examples of the brilliance of ethical and intellectual leadership history in precolonial Southern Africa. It has provided an insight into the development of Mohlomi's philosophies' orientations, intellectual influences, and aspirations, which shaped his life, career, and scholarship. It has located his teachings and works within Basotho's ethical and intellectual history during precolonial Southern Africa. It has discussed his contribution to endogenous knowledge production in Africa by locating his works within the enterprise of African socioethical and political thought (philosophy) that he advocated and became the face of in Southern Africa. It is hoped that beyond sentiments and hagiography, this paper has shown that Mohlomi is a truly a model for post-colonial Africa's ethical leadership and intelligentsia, with strong and insightful perspectives and an uncompromising position on major issues confronting the society of his time which still haunt modern-day African society. For his wisdom, courage, commitment, and integrity, Mohlomi deserves our profound recognition for showing the way to imagine a liberated future for the precolonial and modern-day Africa.

References

Arbousset T. and Daumas F. 1846. *Narrative of an Exploratory Tour of the North-East of the Colony of the Cape of Good Hope.* Cape Town: AS Robertson.

Asquith M. [2006] 2010. *An Autobiography—Two Volumes in One.* London: Hard Press Publishing.

Ayittey, G. 2012. We Let Africa Down Badly. https://seunfakze.wordpress.com/2012/02/15/we-let-africa-down-badly-by-prof-george-n-ayittey/.

Cunningham J. A. and Koski-Jännes A. 2019. The last 10 years: any changes in perceptions of the seriousness of alcohol, cannabis, and substance use in Canada?. *Substance Abuse Treatment, Prevention and Policy* 14 (54):1–6.

Damane M. 1976. The History of Basotho People as expressed through indigenous Poetry or Lithoko. *Unpublished Article*, Maseru, Lesotho.

Du Preez M. 2004. *Of Warriors, Lovers, and Prophets: Unusual Stories from South Africa's Past.* Cape Town: Zebra Press.

Du Preez M. 2003. *Pale Native: Memories of a Renegade Reporter.* Cape Town: Zebra Press.

Ellenberger D. F. and Macgregor J. C. [1912] 1992. *History of the Basotu: Ancient and Modern. London: Caxton (reprinted Morija).*

Epprecht M. 1992. Women, Class and Politics in Colonial Lesotho 1930–1965. *Ph.D. dissertation,* Dalhousie University, Canada.

Fry D. and Elliot SP. 2017. Understanding the linkages between violence against women and violence against children. *The Lancet Global Health* 5 (5): E472-E473.

Gill S. 1993. *A Short History of Lesotho.* Morija: Morija Museum and Archives.

Guma S. M. 1967. *The Form, Content, and Technique of Traditional Literature in Southern Sotho.* Pretoria: van Schaik.

Guma S. M. 1960. *Morena Mohlomi, Mor'a Monyane.* Pietermaritzburg: Shuter and Shooter.

Huxley A. [1954] 2004. *The Doors of Perception and Heavens and Hell.* London: Harper Perennial.

Isiko A. P. 2019. An Expository Study of Witchcraft among the Basoga of Uganda. *International Journal of Humanities Social Sciences and Education* 6 (12): 83–96.

Juma L. 2011. The Laws of Lerotholi: Role and Status of Codified Rules of Custom in the Kingdom of Lesotho. *Pace International Law Review* 23 (1): 2–145.

Junod H.A. 1912. *The Life of a South African Tribe.* Neuchatel, Switzerland: Attinger Bros.

Kennedy B. R. 2017. Global Perspective on Violence of Women and Children: Advocacy on Preventing 21 Century Slavery. *BRK Global Healthcare Journal* 1(1): 1–20.

Livingstone D. 1857. *Missionary Travels and Research in South Africa.* London: John Murray.

Machobane, L. B. B. J. 1978. Mohlomi: Doctor, Traveller, and Sage. *Mohlomi, Journal of Southern African Historical Studies* 2: 5–27.

Macgregor J. C. [1905] 1945 *Basuto Traditions.* Cape Town: Willem Hinddingh Reprint Series No.12

Mahao N. L. 1993. Chieftaincy and the Search for relevant constitutional and institutional models in Lesotho. *Lesotho Law Journal* 9 (1):149–169

Mahao N. L. 2010. O se re ho morwa 'morwa towe! African jurisprudence exhumed. *XLIII CILSA* 317–336.

Matthews S. 2004. Post-development theory and the question of alternatives: a view from Africa. *Third World Quarterly,* 25(2) 373–384.

Mbiti J. S.1990. *African Religions and Philosophy.* Oxford: Heinemann Educational Publishers.

Mbiti J. S. 1991. *Introduction to African Religion.* New York: Heinemann International Inc.

Mofuoa K.V. 2014. Educating African leaders about the Ideals of leadership: Lessons from Mohlomi, the African Philosopher. In: Kondlo K (ed.) *Perspectives of Thought leadership for Africa's Renewal.* Oxford: African Books Collective, 86–109.

Mofuoa K. 2015. The Exemplary Ethical Leadership of King Moshoeshoe of Basotho of Lesotho in the Nineteenth-Century Southern Africa. *Journal of Public Administration and Governance* 5(3): 21–35.

Mofuoa K. 2016. Prospering in the southern Africa's VUCA world of the nineteenth century: A case of resilience of Basotho of Lesotho. *Journal of Enterprising Communities.* 10 (2): 164–177.

Mofuoa K. 2021. Chief Mohlomi: A Mosotho Model of Ethics and Morality in Public Administration and Governance. *Journal of Public Administration and Governance* 11(1): 128–143.

Mokhehle N .1976. *Moshoeshoe 1 Profile See-Moshoeshoe.* Maseru: Mmoho Publications.

Müller C. and Sanderson S. 2020. Witch hunts: A global problem in the 21st century. https://www.dw.com/en/witch-hunts-a-global-problem-in-the-21st-century/a-54495289 (Accessed 20 January 2021).

Mufuzi F. 2014. The Practice of Witchcraft and the Changing Patterns of its Paraphernalia in the Light of Technologically Produced Goods as Presented by Livingstone Museum, 1930s–1973. *Zambia Social Science Journal*, 5 (1): 50–71.

Nadel S. F. 1952. Witchcraft in Four African Societies: An Essay in Comparison. In *Cultures and Societies of Africa.* New York: Random House.

Nicolaides A. and Duho K. C.T. 2019. "Effective Leadership in Organizations: African Ethics and Corruption. *Modern Economy* 10: 1713–1743.

Okonkwo U. U., Eze V. O., Ukaogo V., Okoye-Ugwu S., and Orabueze F. O. 2021. Gender Disparities in Witchcraft Beliefs: A Challenge to Nigerian and African Historiography. *Journal of International Women's Studies* 22 (1): 446–464.

Ohiorhenuam J. F. E. 2009. Don't cry for me Africa: preamble of a memo to the African Prince. *Transition* 102:140–155.

Ortiz-Ospina E. and Roser M. 2017. Violence against children and children's rights. OurWorldInData.org. Available at: https://ourworldindata.org/violence-against-rights-for-children (Accessed, 27 January 2021).

Parrinder E. G. 1954. *African Traditional Religion.* London: Hutchinson's University Library.

Peach L. J. 2002. *Women and World Religions.* Upper Saddle River: Prentice Hall.

Peltzer K. and Phaswana-Mafuya N. 2018. Drug use among youth and adults in a population-based survey in South Africa. *South African Journal of Psychiatry*, 24(0): 1–6.

Procevska O. 2010. Powerlessness, Lamentation and Nostalgia: Discourses of the Post-Soviet Intelligentsia in Modern Latvia. In: Basov N, Simit GF, van Andel J, Mahlonolo S and Netshandama V (eds.) *The Intellectual: A Phenomenon in Multidimensional Perspectives* Oxford, UK: Inter-Disciplinary Press, 47–56.

Purvis J. P. 1909. *Through Uganda to Mt. Elgon.* London: Fisher Unwin.

Quarmyne M. 2011. Witchcraft: A Human Rights Conflict Between Customary/Traditional Laws and the Legal Protection of Women in Contemporary Sub-Saharan Africa. *William & Mary Journal of Race, Gender and Social Justice*, 17 (2): 475–507.

Ray B. C. 1976). *African Religions: Symbol, Ritual, and Community.* New York: Prentice Hall Printers.

Sanders P. 1975. *Moshoeshoe, Chief of the Sotho.* London: Heinemann.

Schapera I. 1938. *A handbook of Tswana Law and Custom*. Oxford: Oxford University Press.

Mothibe T. 2002. State and Society, 1824–1833. *In: Pule N and Thabane M (eds.,) Essays on Aspects of the Political Economy of Lesotho 1500–2000*, Department of History, NUL: Morija Printing Works.

Thompson L. 1975. *Survival in Two Worlds: Moshoeshoe of Lesotho 1786–1870*. Oxford: The Clarendon Press.

Transparency International. 2021. CPI 2020: Sub-Saharan Africa. https://www.transparency.org/en/news/cpi-2020-sub-saharan-africa (Accessed 11 February 2021).

Van der Merwe N. J. 1975. Cannabis Smoking in 13–14th Century Ethiopia. In: Rubin V (ed.) *Cannabis and Culture*. The Hague: Mouton.

Vedder H. 1966. *South West Africa in Early Times*. New York: Barnes & Noble.

Walton J. 1963. The Dagga Pipes of Southern Africa. *Research of National Museum* 1: 85–113.

Ethical Obligation for Research Universities to Expand Access to Essential Medicines

Sarah Jordan Reif and Madeline Chung[1]

Introduction

Approximately one-third of the global population lacks access to life-saving medicines, with nearly 100 million people pushed into extreme poverty seeking treatment (Roth et al., 2018; Hazel, 2021). The cost of essential medicines markedly contributes to the life-threatening gaps in accessibility between the Global North and Global South (Hazel, 2021, Grover et al., 2012). Meanwhile, the research-based pharmaceutical sector is one of the most profitable markets in the world. Global pharmaceutical sales were $768 billion in 2016 and are expected to reach $1.5 trillion by 2023 (Hazel, 2021).

Most medical research in the US is conducted at universities with public funding. University licensing agreements with pharmaceutical companies can play a fundamental role in monopolies and price-gouging, rendering medicines unaffordable. It is imperative that these research institutions prioritize the public health benefits of medical innovation over financial profits to ensure medicines are accessible to global citizens (Hoen, 2003).

We are part of a team of students representing the Case Western Reserve University (CWRU) Partners In Health Engage (PIHE) and Universities Allied for Essential Medicines (UAEM) who have been leading collaborations with the CWRU Technology Transfer Office (TTO) to ensure that

1 The authors are thankful for the support from other CWRU Partners In Health Engage (PIHE) members who helped research and develop the Essential Medicines Equity Framework for the CWRU Technology Transfer Office (TTO), which was made possible with research from the Report Card Project developed by Universities Allied for Essential Medicines (UAEM). The authors are especially grateful for help from Sarah Mathew and Avaneesh Thoudoju for their efforts, research, and writing contributions in the sections entitled Global Implications of Licensing and Moral Duties and a Call to Action for All Global North Institutions, respectively. The authors thank Clara Harb for her significant help in the final review and editing process. The authors are further appreciative of Johana Canari, Lauren Roming, Sarah Zigo, Stephanie Sipics, Tram Phan, and Amber Akhter for their contributions to our work with CWRU's TTO and developing the Essential Medicines Equity Framework for the CWRU TTO, and all the members of the CWRU community and outside affiliates who reviewed and provided feedback on the Framework.

licensing standards are equitable. Categorized as an "R1: Doctoral University" under the Carnegie Basic Classification framework, CWRU is among institutions of higher education holding the highest level of recognition for having "very high research activity" and "at least $5 million in total research expenditures" (Basic Classification Description). As students in medicine, bioethics, biology, and public health at a major research university in the Global North, we believe there is an ethical obligation to both advance the development of biomedical technologies and to ensure these life-saving research products become universally accessible and affordable.

In this paper, we utilize an interdisciplinary approach to understand how history contextualizes our current reality, the importance of lived experiences, and our ethical obligation to adopt the policy recommendations and practices outlined in this paper in order to improve health outcomes locally and globally. We will (1) review a brief history of global health; (2) argue for the ethical duty for institutions to adopt equitable licensing standards; (3) standardize a framework for utilization across research universities; and (4) demonstrate the global health implications of improving access to essential medicines.

Historical Background on Global Health

For centuries, global healthcare was considered a product of missionary and colonial medicine through the lens of Christianity. Protestant tradition sent physicians to the "New World"—land that was illegally stolen from over 100 million indigenous populations through settler colonialism—to open dispensaries and tend to the poor. These efforts were also extended to the Caribbean and China (Grundmann, 1990). This general history overlooks that independent health centers were the norm in the Middle East and parts of Latin America centuries before the 1700s because, as Haitian anthropologist Michel-Rolph Trouillot detailed, "history is the fruit of power," as told by the winners, the colonizers (Trouillot, 1995). We think this brief, albeit insufficient, history of missionary health is central to understanding global health injustice today, especially the lack of robust healthcare infrastructure.

Missionary health was intimately intertwined with international health efforts to control epidemics across countries in the 19th–20th centuries (Brown et al., 2006). Global health initiatives, considering the health of people rather than borders, developed later in the 20th century. Increased globalization (social, economic, and political interdependence) facilitates the dissemination of technologies (contraception, communication, and potable water), human rights standards, infectious disease, conflict, and other threats which exacerbate poverty (Yach & Bettcher, 1998).

Globalization impacted the way international health and global health were conceptualized and operationalized. The transition from international to global health promoted a shift to frame health in terms of equity (Beaglehole & Bonita, 2010). Partners In Health—and its founders, Paul Farmer, Jim Yong Kim, Ophelia Dahl, and other colleagues—work(ed) tirelessly to decolonize global health from its imperial roots in favor of a biosocial approach that incorporates medicine with anthropology, sociology, history, ethics, and political economy (Farmer et al., 2013). In doing so, global health's powerful role in disease mitigation shifted toward social justice to recognize the role of power in illness and health.

Pharmacology and science are required to develop and manufacture medications but play a lesser role to power and profit in terms of accessing biomedical technology and medicines. We can turn to bioethics to understand our obligation to improve universal access to essential medicines. As we are all based in the United States, our obligations refer to those of the Global North where advanced biomedical research and exclusive licensing are rampant.

Long-Standing Issues in Access Viewed through the Lens of Bioethics

In the 1960s–70s, hemodialysis, mechanical ventilation, artificial nutrition, and other biomedical innovations were discovered to prolong human life. Medical teams were tasked with deciding who had access and how much life-sustaining treatment was ethical. Simultaneously, journalists published accounts of unethical research, including the Tuskegee Syphilis Study and the Stanford Prison Experiment. Together, these factors formalized a new discipline, bioethics, to answer questions about life and death and to better operationalize the Hippocratic Oath's demand to do no harm (Jonsen, 1991).

In 1979, Tom Beauchamp and James Childress developed principles for biomedical ethics to help dissect ethical issues in medicine, including autonomy, beneficence, non-maleficence, and justice. *Autonomy* states that people who have agency and liberty ought to be able to make their own medical decisions. *Beneficence* is the obligation for healthcare workers to do good by their patients by acting in their best interest. *Non-maleficence* requires that practitioners avoid harm to their patients. *Justice* considers how benefits and burdens are distributed to a population.

These principles have served as a guiding model for determining standards for animal research and drug trials, monitored by the US government, thereby setting a precedent for government intervention to ensure safety and equity through the development process of new biomedical technologies (Menikoff et al., 2017). All four principles, most notably justice, can be applied to our concerns about exclusive licensing and patents for essential medicines. First, by our evaluation, "essential" medicines—including insulin, chemotherapy, immunotherapy, antiretroviral therapy, and tuberculosis regimens, among others—provide extended quality years of life. If a medicine is offered to a patient with the best American health insurance, it ought to be considered essential.

As the field of bioethics emerged, philosopher John Rawls introduced a concept on what he called the "Veil of Ignorance." This thought experiment compels an individual to consider what social support they would want provided if they did not know their class, race, ethnicity, gender, religion, and so forth (Rawls, 1971). Scholars agree that the Veil of Ignorance indicates countries have an obligation to ensure positive rights—to provide essential healthcare (Korobkin, 1998; Fritz and Cox, 2019). Using Rawls' framework, there is a clear beneficent and non-maleficent obligation for people with power to prioritize the provision of fundamental human rights.

Nativism, racism, and neoliberalism prevent solidarity-based approaches in favor of individualism. Yet, for centuries, societies founded their policies on the idea of providing the best outcome for most of their population. Most countries in the Global North countries, with the exception of the US, have a national healthcare system because they value the principles of access, justice, and accountability. In the US, individual autonomy is prioritized over social justice and collective well-being. However, people cannot act autonomously without access to all available options. The liberty component of autonomy is restricted because there is no "independence from controlling influences" (Beauchamp & Childress, 2019). Inadequate power and resources control the decision. By limiting access to life-saving treatments, we are stripping autonomy from millions of people, thus making our protection of the principle inconsequential. We can adopt a consequentialist approach—similar to the justification for national health systems in other countries—to prioritize equitable access to essential medicines over the profits of a few politicians, high-level executives, and shareholders.

Justice Considerations for Global Health Authorities Beyond Universities

With over 450 million cases, including six million deaths worldwide, the response to COVID-19 has been a race of unprecedented speed and unrelenting international research efforts to transition this disease from life-threatening to vaccine-preventable. Although the World Health Organization (WHO) announced that countries representing 64% of the world's population made legally binding commitments to buy and fairly distribute COVID-19 vaccines globally, we have still seen a vaccine apartheid unfold with a surplus of vaccines in the Global North and an insufficient number in the Global South. World leaders have failed to facilitate the equitable distribution and access to publicly funded, life-saving vaccines, ultimately forgoing justice in times of a pandemic and revealing an unacceptably high level of moral negligence.

In order to protect individuals and communities from emerging health threats, world leaders must develop protective measures and procedures taken by state and local health authorities that are ethical, legal, and effective. The devastating consequences on individuals, families, and communities due to weak infectious disease infrastructure cannot be ignored any longer (Lagay, 2004; Margolis, 2001). While outbreaks are sometimes unpreventable, the danger becomes far greater when they are left uncontrolled and unmanaged (CDC, 2015). Failure to "meet the minimum capabilities . . . for readiness" can cause health hazards from emerging infectious diseases to become epidemics, or even pandemics, resulting in unnecessary and largely preventable deaths, especially for those from our most vulnerable communities (Mayer, 2009).

All people are susceptible to contracting COVID-19, but that does not mean the disease is non-discriminatory. The pandemic has highlighted that individuals with a low socioeconomic status (SES) experience a disproportionate burden of disease since they have restricted access to medical care. Despite the economic growth of the last century, the global distribution of wealth remains intentionally unbalanced due to many systemic injustices including colonialism (now neo-colonialism), through which continued resource and labor exploitation are rampant, widening gaps in access to healthcare, education, potable water, healthy and affordable food options, and sanitary environments (Jones, 2010). Lack of access to other essential supplies increases transmission and mortality risk for COVID-19 among other diseases and pathological conditions that have their own unique comorbidities (Beauchamp & Childress, 2012).

Moreover, low SES is deeply intertwined with race, ethnicity, education level, citizenship status, and immigration status because societies have been built on the exploitation of the minority groups which experience these covariates most often. Populations at high risk for COVID-19 exposure and mortality have been forced to endure the systemic injustices that actively work to oppress racial and ethnic minority groups. This oppression includes "long-standing racial bias in health care—including the dismissal of legitimate concerns and symptoms—that can help explain poor [health] outcomes even in the case of black [people] with the most advantages" (Villarosa, 2018).

Although COVID-19 has helped shed light on the "deep fault-lines in our medical system...that stratify health care along lines of race, class, age, and disability," properly combating public health threats aggravated by systemic injustice necessitates significant mobilization of resources and international cooperation (Ginsburg et al., 2020). These collaborations can help ensure equitable and ethical medical resource distribution for the people who are the most urgently at risk for infection and death with more limited access to treatment or safety measures. Marginalized people have a right to high-quality healthcare, and under-prioritizing them during a global pandemic is a serious threat to their chance of survival (Beauchamp & Childress, 2012).

Therefore, as demonstrated most recently by this pandemic, our world's primary justice consideration must first and foremost speak to protecting the most vulnerable lives from the most disadvantaged nations. Global leaders must adopt a sense of duty and moral obligation to combat the disproportionate burden of disease and death by implementing legislative policies that would improve access to and affordability of medicines for populations who face vulnerability, exploitation, and discrimination.

When health disparities and issues of justice get overlooked or dismissed by the very leaders who claim to be advocates of health equity and social justice, then the goal of providing equitable access to life-saving vaccines and other essential medicines cannot be achieved. Although neoliberalism and contemporary ideas associated with free-market capitalism have made efforts to support vulnerable populations unpopular, now is the time to set a precedent of solidarity and stand firm in our obligation to protect the lives that have, for so long, been forgotten and left behind.

Biomedical Licensing and Barriers to Optimal Health in the US

In the US, nearly one in four people cannot afford healthcare, despite the fact that this country is home to many hubs of pharmaceutical development (Kaiser Family Foundation, 2019). Access is worse in the Global South due to people facing physical inaccessibility to medications as well as generally lower incomes. As reviewed in our brief history of global health delivery, lack of access to medicines is a consequence of colonialism due to inadequate and unsustainable healthcare infrastructure (Kettler et al., 2020; Bigdeli et al., 2013).

Without investment in "stuff, staff, space, and systems"—as promoted by the founders of Partners In Health—many low-income people rely on informal paths to access healthcare resources (Mills et al., 2002; Building Strong Health Systems, 2021). Of all healthcare costs, medicines account for 20–60% of health spending in low- and middle-income countries, with 50-90% of these expenses being billed as out-of-pocket costs, placing an undue burden on already vulnerable populations (Cameron et al., 2009; WHO, 2004; Bigdeli et al., 2013). In Table I, we frame how the cost of medicines affects all five levels of health systems (Bigdeli et al., 2013). These barriers essentially serve to impact the way medicines are licensed and patented, thereby either promoting or restricting access.

There are a host of mechanisms, detailed in an investigation by the US Congressional Research Service, that pharmaceutical companies and institutions use to increase profit, limit competition, and extend monopolies (Richards et al., 2020). Pharmaceutical patents, a form of exclusive licensing for innovation and production, are typically awarded in the US for twenty years from the date of patent filing, and similar licensing policies exist throughout the Global North. Through the 1980 Bayh-Dole Act, American universities gained financial incentives to commercialize innovation and support pharmaceutical profits (Ouellette & Tutt, 2020). Moreover, patent holders can repackage old research products or make minor modifications (such as making changes to the form or dosage) to perpetuate their patent when, in fact, it did not require true innovation. This technique is known as "evergreening," a practice which not only increases prices, but also solidifies monopolies.

Manufacturers also promote "product hopping," which is defined as removing an old product or introducing a new, but similar product as a new patent with a later date, thus extending the exclusive licensing agreement. Repeated "evergreening" and "product hopping" leads to "patent thickets," thereby limiting space for generics. Further, companies can negotiate "Pay-for-Delay" agreements by offering settlements to other companies to delay releasing a generic alternative. On average, there were 125 patent applications filed for each of the top twelve grossing medications of 2017; approximately seventy-one patents were successfully issued for each, blocking nearly forty years of competition (Initiative for Medicines, Access, and Knowledge, 2020). No statutes exist in the US to forbid these tactics and global initiatives spearheaded by non-governmental organizations lack enforcement.

Table I

Barriers to accessing medicines categorized by health system level.

Extrapolated from Bigdeli et al. article and table on strengths and weaknesses of existing frameworks (2012).

Level of health system	Barriers to accessing medicines
Individual, household and community	Cost of medicines and services
Health service delivery	High medicine prices
	Irrational prescription and dispensing
Health sector	Pharmaceutical sector governance
	Medicines price control
Public policies cutting across sectors	Low public accountability and transparency
	Low priority attached to social sectors
	Conflict between trade and economic goals for pharmaceutical markets and public health goals
International and regional level	Unethical use of patents and intellectual property rights
	Distorted research and development, not targeting disease burden in low- and middle-income countries

Another practice, previously invisible to many people across the world, is the effect of licensing on access to COVID-19 vaccines compounded with the implications of institutionalized racism. In October 2021, Moderna Therapeutics refused to share their vaccine recipe; in response, the WHO hired a biotechnical company in South Africa to reverse engineer it (Aizenman, 2021; Maxmen, 2022). The South African company succeeded in replicating the vaccine in February 2022, paving the way for increased vaccination rates on the continent (Maxmen, 2022). While Moderna agreed to not enforce intellectual property rights—at least during the pandemic—by refusing to disclose the vaccine's ingredients, the company is prioritizing their profits over the health and well-being of people during a public health emergency, further inflating global transmission and mortality rates.

To further expand on the context and consequences of these actions, it is essential to note that in 2019, Moderna's revenue was $60 million, and in 2021, they were projected to generate at least $20 billion (Robbins, 2021). Additionally, from a comparative perspective, while the United Kingdom had succeeded in vaccinating 85% of its population by December 2021, only 6% of the continent of Africa had completed a full, two-dose vaccine regimen (Ivanova, 2021). This reality is known as a *vaccine apartheid* because it communicates how the disparity is a direct result of intentional decisions around power, profit, and medicinal access.

In addition to making biomedical licensing more equitable, efforts must be made to implement large social investments, such as appropriate financial reparations, which work to address centuries of colonization and oppression. For example, in a study done by medical anthropologists comparing COVID-19 transmission rates in Louisiana and South Korea, researchers found that if descendants of enslaved people in the US had been recipients of financial reparations in the years prior to the COVID-19 pandemic, transmission rates in Louisiana could have been 31–68% lower (Richardson, et al., 2021). Reparations can help develop generational wealth, which ultimately allows people to experience greater opportunities for access to healthcare. Social investments, outside of improving biomedical licensing, are crucial to both acknowledging historical violations of human rights and directly seeking to improve quality of life.

Global Health Implications of Licensing

The urgency of addressing licensing issues cannot be separated from their global health implications. Therefore, it is important to discuss the threats to public health and well-being when we fail to take these negative tradeoffs into consideration, highlighted by current issues with the prescription medications Xtandi, Daraprim, dt4, and the recently developed COVID-19 vaccine.

Xtandi is a treatment for late-stage prostate cancer that was developed at the University of California Los Angeles (UCLA) in the early 2000s. Although Xtandi is the only medication available to the 1.5 million people diagnosed with prostate cancer in India, it is priced at over forty times the average per capita income, making it inaccessible to those who need it most. UCLA sold its royalty interests to Royalty Pharmaceuticals and Japanese-based pharmaceutical company, Astellas (Hampton, 2016). The university then filed a patent claim on its ~43% royalty share which was denied by the Indian Patent Office (Mukherjee, 2016). Mumbai-based BDR Pharma produced an affordable alternative, threatening the profits of Xtandi, leading UCLA to appeal the patent denial to the high court.

UCLA must be held accountable by accepting profit cuts and increasing the accessibility of Xtandi to millions. Their goals, which revolve around leadership in research, grants, and patents, are incompatible with their current practice of prioritizing profit over the lives of people with prostate cancer (Stout et al., 2018). Additionally, large, networked institutions like UCLA set the precedent for patent royalties in partnerships, given that nearly 25% of the 252 medications approved by the Food and Drug Administration (FDA) between 1998 and 2007 were initially developed at universities (Panditrao & Aditi Mridul, 2017).

Pharmaceutical lobbyists in the US Congress also play a major role in limiting biomedical licensing regulation. Turing Pharmaceuticals CEO, Martin Shkreli, increased the price of Daraprim, an HIV medication, by 5000% overnight and hired lobbyists to combat the congressional outreach and public outcry against drug pricing alterations that ensued. The pharmaceutical industry heavily fortifies federal lobbying in Congress (including $300 million in campaign donations) to ensure medicine costs do not decrease, even with major insurance reforms like the Affordable Care Act (CREW, 2018; Geubert & Bubela, 2014).

Profit-seeking behaviors are preventing people around the world from receiving healthcare and life-saving therapies. In South Africa, the country with the highest number of new HIV/AIDS infections annually, pharmaceutical profits are prioritized over the health of millions (Laher et al., 2020). Despite the incidence of the disease, less than 1% of the HIV positive population in SA receive proper care due to overwhelming financial barriers. In the 1980s, Yale University developed the antiretroviral medication, d4T, and negotiated a patent agreement with Bristol-Myers Squibb (BMS) that would have resulted in a high cost barrier once this product hit the market (Borger & Boseley, 2001). However, due to pressure from negative media attention organized by student advocates, Yale-BMS decreased the cost of d4T in SA to 1/34th of its original price (Post, 2003).

In Latin America, Pfizer Pharmaceutical, which was providing vaccines to the region, demanded that Brazil and Argentina put up assets such as military bases as collateral to cover any legal fees Pfizer could incur from civil suits or negligence accusations during vaccine dissemination (Davies, 2021). Similar abuse of power exists in Colombia, where the government paid $27–30 per dose for Moderna vaccines while the US paid $15–16 per dose (Robbins, 2021). These events, among others, culminated in government officials releasing statements expressing how they felt as though they were being "held for ransom" for daring to gain access to life-saving vaccines for their populations (Davies, 2021). Soon thereafter, Pfizer announced that they would collaborate with a Brazilian pharmaceutical company to manufacture vaccines for the region (Pfizer, 2021).

Even though this action is a step in the right direction, Pfizer's decision to help manufacture more vaccines in the region was likely an effort to escape negative press, thereby reaffirming their power in this twisted dynamic. It is these systemic, intentional decisions made by manufacturers without accountability that cause and perpetuate vaccine apartheid and other instances of global health injustice.

Collaborating with TTOs to Improve Licensing Standards

Renowned research institutions maintain a high magnitude of innovation and experimental processes required to further research and development. Since the 1970s, the Carnegie Classification of Institutions has categorized universities based on degrees awarded and research expenditure (Basic Classification Description). R1 (very high research activity) and R2 (high research activity) schools are doctoral universities which award at least 20 doctoral degrees in a given year and receive at least $5 million in total research expenditure as reported by the National Science Foundations (Basic Classification Description).

These schools have the stuff, staff, space, and systems to conduct high-level biomedical research with the potential to treat and cure disease and disability. As such, R1 and R2 institutions must lead equitable framing initiatives. These schools have the most interaction with pharmaceutical and manufacturing companies and, thus, the most power to improve access. The licensing standards and contracts negotiated with pharmaceutical companies are what ultimately determine pricing, length of monopoly, and competition. We will review how currently intellectual property standards threaten essential medicine access and how constituents of R1 and R2 universities can collaborate with technology transfer offices to improve licensing standards.

Innovation, as intellectual property (IP), is often patented so that it can be protected. However, protecting IP over access to necessary health care is antithesis to the stated values of most R1 and R2 schools. Universities are guided by pillars of engagement, integrity, and stewardship, seeking to improve the lives of people around the world. However, their actions within the realm of biomedical advances may not always reflect this sentiment. By not taking aggressive, intentional action to improve biomedical licensing, universities are falling short of the goals and commitments they have outlined in their missions.

Due to the substantial role of universities in developing biomedical technology, managing IP responsibly can improve access to medical innovations globally (Hoen, 2003). Moreover, most of this research is funded by American taxes through National Institute of Health (NIH) grants. NIH funding has contributed to every medication—210 in total—approved by the FDA between 2010-2016 (Cleary, et al., 2018; Mamidi, 2021). Yet, there is not widespread access to medicines, nor does the US believe there ought to be universal healthcare, distinguishing itself from the rest of the world with its fatal individualism complex.

A university's groundbreaking research can only enrich and improve people's lives insofar as it is affordable and accessible to those who need it. Concerned that our university was not fulfilling its obligation to make technology accessible, we organized meetings with the TTO to develop a greater understanding of how the office makes negotiations with manufacturing companies and secures licensing agreements for research products made at the university. As students, we felt an obligation to (1) understand our own university's policies and practices as it relates to limited access and (2) advocate that we promote justice and universal access to healthcare. Figure I outlines our general process for engaging with university TTOs and recommending licensing improvements.

During the initial meetings with TTOs, student leadership groups will focus on acquiring a stronger understanding of the office's main goals, interests, and hesitations with biomedical licensing. After engaging in these conversations and establishing a relationship with the TTO, students can work on outlining their main concerns surrounding any lack of transparency in the licensing process, insufficient exploration and use of non-exclusive licensing alternatives, and inadequate oversight on manufacturing companies with whom we have agreements.

Given the precedent of exclusive licensing as the standard for awarding innovation, many TTOs may have the misguided belief that, without

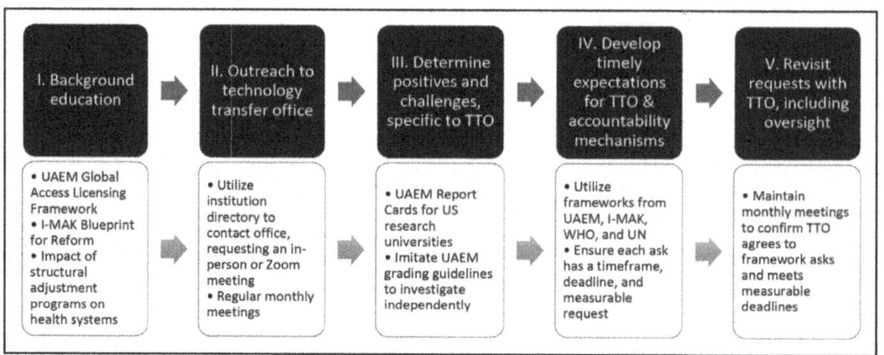

Figure I. *Overview of the process used to engage with TTOs at research institutions.*

patents, we would not have biomedical technology advancement. Conversations with TTOs should also determine the level of support and interest in changing the licensing *status quo.* Offices may verbally acknowledge equity as an important consideration, but delay or refuse adoption of alternative licensing practices. TTOs, at the minimum, should be receptive to meeting with university students and being transparent about their licensing standards. Excellent TTOs will consider recommendations from students and alter policies for maximum transparency and accountability. Figure II indicates common discourses of delay that TTOs will use to limit or prolong licensing changes.

Prior to, and throughout meetings with TTOs, students will need to be responsible for conducting their own independent research on licensing policies. UAEM produces report cards outlining positive actions and areas for improvement for leading American research universities. They also author the UAEM Evidence Wordpress blog to collate information and evidence in support for alternatives to exclusive licensing (UAEM Evidence). We heavily relied on this research and interdisciplinary discussions with other health organizers around the country.

Based on our experience working with TTOs, we developed a framework explaining the biomedical licensing process and areas for improvement. We highly recommend this approach for other institutions, as it can help educate the university, raise awareness, outline university accomplishments and areas of concern, and list institution-specific action items to improve access. We have included general categories related to licensing and sample action steps and practices that R1 and R2 institutions would be able to adopt if they are truly committed to addressing the outstanding issues that shape and are shaped by access to biomedical innovations (Table II). These policies and guidelines were developed using the UAEM report card grades which rate research institutions' commitment to transparency, equitable licensing, research for neglected health needs, and student empowerment.

Table II

Policy recommendations and action items for R1 and R2 universities. These can be adapted to be university-specific and incorporated into a framework presented to the technology transfer office. The items should be prioritized and include expected timelines and measures for accountability.

General Policy Recommendations	Specific Action Steps and Practices
Publicly support UAEM's Equitable Technology Access Framework	Waive market and data exclusivities when at all possible. This includes abstaining from applying for extensions on market and data protections. Promotion of these exclusivities can often block or delay competition and thus increase monopolies and cost. The Food and Drug Administration permits up to 5 years of exclusivity for most small molecules that have not previously been approved. This length should never be exceeded, unless by the discovery of a drug to treat an orphan condition (fewer than 200,000 individuals in the US), at which 7 years of exclusivity is permitted (Hennebry, 2018).
	Increased transparency about meetings with manufacturers and pharmaceutical companies. Notes should be taken during these meetings to record concerns and agreements. Notes should be made available.
	All (most likely, but not limited to, federal) funding sources and amounts should be disclosed in annual reports and made available online. This includes the amount of funding for the research and development process with markers indicating the use of the funds. Given the necessity of grant proposals, researchers should be able to easily compile an itemized list of funding.
	Include step-in rights: Universities should be able to intervene and alter or end the agreement with a manufacturer if they are not meeting the obligations of the agreement. This can ensure higher equity standards are included and being met.
Publicly support at least one COVID-19 open technology framework	• Open COVID Pledge (OCP) • Coronavirus Technology Access Pool (C-TAP) • Stanford/Harvard/MIT COVID-19 Technology Access Framework

General Policy Recommendations	Specific Action Steps and Practices
Transparency about technology transfer negotiation process	More disclosure about the processes, funding, goals, and outcomes within the technology transfer office. A public website should include more information about how commercialization of university intellectual property is conducted and approved.
	Answers to the following questions are a start to outline the technology transfer process: • How does the office seek out manufacturers and pharmaceutical companies to license technology to? • What, if any, standards are set for these companies? • How does the university decide whether licensing will be pursued for an innovation or product? • How does the university decide with whom this licensing agreement will be made? • How does the university monitor compliance with the licensing agreement? • What decisions by manufacturers and pharmaceutical companies will not be tolerated? • When is information shared with the university/public about licensing agreements? • Does the amount of public money invested in the product impact licensing decisions? • What amount of transparency is required from manufacturers and pharmaceutical companies?
Include people outside the technology transfer office in licensing negotiations	The technology transfer office should include at least one undergraduate and two graduate students (if possible, one from medical school and one from law school) in the licensing review process. These students will be able to raise concerns about the equity of an agreement and their opinions should hold equal power.
Ensure accountability and regular follow-up meetings	The technology transfer office should seek out, agree to, and continue collaborations with students and interested entities. This should include, at least, 3 meetings per year to review updates. The university should mandate reporting for all clinical trial results and funding.

General Policy Recommendations	Specific Action Steps and Practices
Ensure obligations are met of current agreement, if applicable. *Many R1 and R2 universities have agreed to a UAEM Global Access Licensing Framework.*	Legally prevent manufacturers and pharmaceutical companies from engaging in tactics that can block generic competition, especially for production in resource-limited countries. The following should not be permitted: • Follow-on patents, including product, process, and use patents. These types of patents promote multiple licensing agreements for incremental developments.
	Other provisions can be included into agreements to promote equity and competition. The following should be included: • At-cost provisions: Licensed technology should be made available for no profit when: (1) "[a] component of the licensed product is too complex to be feasible for replication and generic production;" and/or (2) "the demand for the product... is too small to induce a generic company to enter the production" (UAEM 2010).
	"Do not seek patents on research platforms, diagnostic tests, and other technologies that can be adapted for commercial use in a short period with little additional investment." (UAEM 2010). • Patent on these types of inventions hinder innovation by adding costly licensing fees and can promote patent thickets
Actively promoting equitable licensing	For all patents, rely on non-exclusive licensing. All rights to the products should be reserved by the university. The product should be shared widely to encourage competition (UAEM 2010).
	Review pending and future license agreements—including students—to limit all exclusive licensing agreements.
	Collaborate with other universities (public and private) to learn best methods for prioritizing non-exclusive licensing, including communication with manufacturers and pharmaceutical companies.

Moral Duties and a Call to Action for All Global North Institutions

We call on R1 and R2 universities to share our process and framework to educate other members of the institution on the urgency and implications of licensing decisions and to pressure administrators to transition away from grandstanding and profit-driven decisions toward real accountability. We

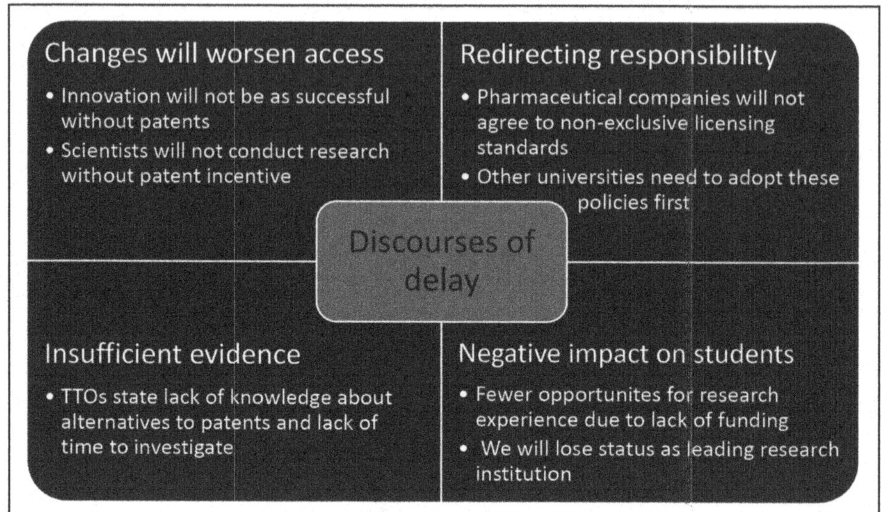

Figure II. *Common discourses of delay from TTOs and universities who are hesitant to transition away from exclusive licensing standards. Adapted from Lamb et al. article and figure on discourses of climate delay (2020).*

urge these biomedical research institutions in the Global North to adopt alternatives to exclusive agreements, such as open-source listing, which makes details of innovation freely available to others in academia and the broader public. In addition to promoting competition, open-source listing also prevents others from patenting the invention, which helps to protect the institution's innovative achievement while also increasing accessibility to a potentially life-saving product.

University research is upstream from the development process. Using an open-source listing model means that there is a chance for early leverage, with blind foresight to predict marketability. In order to effectively fight against limited accessibility to life-saving medicines, universities need to acknowledge that research is intended to meet public needs, including health care advancements. As such, global public health concerns should be considered in the patenting and licensing process.

Research universities across the Global North need to reassess their role in promoting or preventing accessible medicines worldwide. Developing biomedical technology is one small part of improving healthcare. Universities are responsible for leading conscious efforts to limit exclusive agreements and make ethical decisions about licensing. While equitable licensing is a clear mechanism for universities to promote global health justice and to hold pharmaceutical companies more accountable, these actions must be adopted in tandem with other efforts which seek to strengthen health systems while also addressing discrimination globally.

Ultimately, the benefits of such an approach can be demonstrated by the events of the COVID-19 pandemic detailed in the Justice Considerations for Global Health Authorities section above. Therefore, in addition to committing to more equitable licensing standards, universities must improve transparency about the process and strive to educate researchers, students, and other members of the institution on the gravity of licensing decisions within the context of global health access.

Conclusion

Global health justice will only advance through collaborations between organizations, disease control authorities, health departments, and ministries of health. These health advocates and leaders must address preventive health practices, infectious disease treatment goals, obstacles to accessing healthcare, and disparities in health outcomes with the knowledge that integrative approaches to healthcare build stronger, more sustainable health infrastructures, and prepare systems for crises.

Together, with community input, these groups can enact effective strategies, address health disparities, offer constructive feedback, and expand support systems. However, when health authorities at the university and global levels fail to prioritize justice and access in their policy decisions and innovation licensing, individuals and populations die from preventable and treatable conditions. Academic biomedical research institutions and governmental bodies around the world must adopt the values of justice by actively addressing the gaps in essential medicine access and affordability.

We recognize that research universities, especially those designated as R1 (very high research activity) and R2 (high research activity), are a small part of a larger system designed for the Global North to profit off the exploitation of the Global South. We hope our framework demonstrates the tangible actions that biomedical institutions must take to fulfill their obligation to the world. These obligations extend past perfunctory pledges and value statements to genuine system-level change and robust mechanisms of accountability. We believe that adopting these general guidelines and specific action steps will provide practical implications for the betterment of humankind. Universities can further use their connections to urge other sectors to invest in global health justice.

Leaders in bioethics, medicine, and public health are some of the loudest voices for change. We urge leaders across these and other disciplines to join us in combating preventable morbidity and mortality, investing in education around the urgency of social justice, and building resiliency to continue the fight for justice. Through these developments we will help our world move through this pandemic to a brighter future with accessible healthcare, potable water, humane housing, fair labor laws, and sincere dedication to addressing the climate crisis.

References

Aizenman, N. 2021. Modern won't share its vaccine recipe. WHO has hired an African startup to crack it. *National Public Radio,* https://www.npr.org/sections/goatsandsoda/2021/10/19/1047411856/the-great-vaccine-bake-off-has-begun.

Basic Classification Description. 2021. *The Carnegie Classification of Institutions of Higher Education,* https://carnegieclassifications.iu.edu/classification_descriptions/basic.php.

Beaglehole, R. & Bonita, R. 2010. What is Global Health? *Global Health Action* 3, https://dx.doi.org/10.3402%2Fgha.v3i0.5142.

Beauchamp, T., & Childress, J. 2019. *Principles of Biomedical Ethics* (8th ed.). Oxford University Press.

Bigdeli, M., Jacobs, B., Tomson, G., Laing, R., Ghaffar, A., Dujardin, B., & Van Damme, W. 2012. Access to medicines from a health system perspective. *Health Policy and Planning* 28(7), 692–704, https://doi.org/10.1093/heapol/czs108.

Borger, J., & Boseley, S. (2001). Conscience Before Profit. *The Guardian,* https://www.theguardian.com/world/2001/mar/13/education.highereducation.

Brown, T., Cueto, M., & Fee, E. 2006. The World Health Organization and the Transition from International to Global Public Health. *American Journal of Public Health* 96(1), 62-72.

Building Strong Health Systems. 2021. *Partners In Health.* https://www.pih.org/our-approach.

Cameron, A., Ewen, M., Ross-Degnan, D., et al. 2009. Medicine prices, availability, and affordability in 36 developing and middle-income countries: A secondary analysis. *Lancet* 373, 240–9, https://doi.org/10.1016/S0140-6736(08)61762-6.

Case Western Reserve University. 2021. Mission, vision, and values: Acting with purpose. https://case.edu/about/mission-vision-values/.

Case Western Reserve University School of Medicine. 2021. Navigation and search: About. https://case.edu/medicine/about.

CDC. 2015. Ebola Virus Disease: Outbreak Preparedness. *Centers for Disease Control and Prevention,* https://www.cdc.gov/vhf/ebola/outbreaks/preparedness/outbreak-preparedness.html.

Cleary, E., Beierlein, J., Khanuja, N., McNamee, L., & Ledley, F. 2018. Contribution of NIH funding to new drug approvals 2010-2016. *Proceedings of the National Academy of Sciences of the United States of America* 115(10), https://doi.org/10.1073/pnas.1715368115.

CREW. 2018. A bitter pill: How big pharma lobbies to keep prescription drug prices high. *Citizens for Responsibility and Ethics in Washington*, https://www.citizensfor-ethics.org/reports-investigations/crew-reports/a-bitter-pill-how-big-pharma-lobbies-to-keep-prescription-drug-prices-high/.

Davies, M., Ruiz, I., Langlois, J., Furneaux, R., & K, X. 2021. "Held to ransom": Pfizer plays hardball in Covid-19 vaccine negotiations with Latin American countries. *STAT*, https://www.statnews.com/2021/02/23/pfizer-plays-hardball-in-covid19-vaccine-negotiations-in-latin-america/.

Farmer, P., Yong Kim, J., Kleinman, A., & Basilico, M. 2013. *Reimagining Global Health: An Introduction*. University of California Press.

Fritz, Z., & Cox, C. 2019. Conflicting demands on a modern healthcare service: Can Rawlsian justice provide a guiding philosophy for the NHS and other socialized health services? *Bioethics* 33(5), 609–616, https://doi.org/10.1111/bioe.12568.

Ginsburg, F., Mills, M. & Rapp, R. 2020. From Quality of Life to Disability Justice: Imagining a Post-Covid Future. *Somatosphere*, http://somatosphere.net/2020/from-quality-of-life-to-disability-justice.html/.

Grover, A., Citro, B., Mankad, M., & Lander, F. 2012. "Pharmaceutical companies and global lack of access to medicines: Strengthening accountability under the right to health." *Journal for Law and Medical Ethics*, 40(2), 234–50, https://doi.org/10.1111/j.1748-720x.2012.00661.x.

Grundmann, C. 1990. Proclaiming the Gospel by Healing the Sick? Historical and Theological Annotations on Medical Mission. *International Bulletin of Mission Research* 14(3), 120–126. https://doi.org/10.1177%2F239693939001400307.

Hampton, P. 2016. UCLA sells royalty rights connected with cancer drug to Royalty Pharma. *The University of California Los Angeles*, https://newsroom.ucla.edu/releases/ucla-sells-royalty-rights-connected-with-cancer-drug-to-royalty-pharma.

Hazel, J. 2021. Why access matters. *Access to Medicine Index*. https://accesstomedicine-foundation.org/access-to-medicine-index/about-the-index/why-access-matters#.

Hoen, E. 2003. TRIPS, Pharmaceutical Patents and Access to Essential Medicines: Seattle, Doha and Beyond. *World Health Organization* 11(8), 39–68, https://www.who.int/intellectualproperty/topics/ip/tHoen.pdf.

Initiative for Medicine, Access, and Knowledge. 2020. Overpatented, overpriced: How excessive pharmaceutical patenting is extending monopolies and driving up drug prices. http://www.i-mak.org/wp-content/uploads/2018/08/I-MAK-Overpatented-Overpriced-Report.pdf.

Ivanova, A. 2021. Vaccine apartheid is prolonging COVID—not vaccine hesitancy. *Open Democracy*, https://www.opendemocracy.net/en/vaccine-apartheid-is-prolonging-covid-not-vaccine-hesitancy/.

Jones, C. M. 2010. The moral problem of health disparities. American journal of public health 100(S1), S47-S51

Jonsen, A. 1991. American Moralism and the Origin of Bioethics in the United States. *The Journal of Medicine and Philosophy* 16, 113–130.

Kaiser Family Foundation. 2019. Poll: Nearly 1 in 4 Americans taking prescription drugs says it's difficult to afford their medicines, including larger shares among those with health issues, with low incomes, and nearing Medicare age. https://www.kff.org/health-costs/press-release/poll-nearly-1-in-4-americans-taking-prescription-drugs-say-its-difficult-to-afford-medicines-including-larger-shares-with-low-incomes/.

Kettler, H., Lehtimaki, S., & Schwalbe, N. 2020. Accelerating access to medicines in a changing world. *Bulletin of the World Health Organization* 98(9), 641–643, https://dx.doi.org/10.2471%2FBLT.19.249664.

Korobkin, R. 1998. Determining health care rights from behind a veil of ignorance. *University of Illinois Law Review* 3, 801–36, https://doi.org/10.2139/ssrn.85189.

Lagay, F. 2004. The Proposed Model State Emergency Health Powers Act. Virtual Mentor 6(5), 224–226.

Laher, F., Bekker, L., Garrett, N., Lazarus, E., & Gray, G. 2020. Review of preventative HIV vaccine clinical trials in South Africa. *Archives of Virology* 165, 2439–2452, https://doi.org/10.1007/s00705-020-04777-2.

Lamb, W., Mattioli, G., Levi, S. Roberts, T., Capstick, S., Creutzig, F., Minx, J., Müller-Hansen, F., Culhane, T., & Steinberger, J. 2020. Discourses of climate delay. *Global Sustainability* 3, e17, https://doi.org/10.1017/sus.2020.13.

Mamidi, A. 2021. The Role of University of California in Access to Medicines. *Davis Political Review,* https://www.davispoliticalreview.com/article/the-role-of-university-of-california-in-access-to-medicines.

Margolis, M. R. 2001. Draft Model State Emergency Health Powers Act Released for Consideration by States, https://www.law.uh.edu/healthlaw/perspectives/PublicHealth/011128Draft.html.

Maxmen, A. 2022. South African scientists copy Moderna's COVID vaccine. *Nature* 602, 372–373, https://doi.org/10.1038/d41586-022-00293-2.

Mayer, E. E. 2009. Prepare for the Worst: Protecting Civil Liberties in the Modern Age of Bioterrorism. Journal of Constitutional Law 11(4), 1051–1076.

Menikoff, J., Kaneshiro, J., & Pritchard, I. 2017. The Common Rule, Updated. *The New England Journal of Medicine* 376, 613–615. https://www.nejm.org/doi/10.1056/NEJMp1700736.

Mukherjee, R. 2016. Patent denied, price of prostate cancer drug may go down. *The Times of India,* https://timesofindia.indiatimes.com/Patent-denied-price-of-prostate-cancer-drug-may-go-down/articleshow/55343339.cms.

Ouellette, L., & Tutt, A. 2020. How do patent incentives affect university researchers? *International Review of Law and Economics* 61, https://doi.org/10.1016/j.irle.2019.105883.

Pfizer. 2021. Pfizer and BioNTech announce collaboration with Brazil's Eurofarma to manufacture COVID-19 vaccine doses for Latin America. https://www.pfizer.com/news/press-release/press-release-detail/pfizer-and-biontech-announce-collaboration-brazils.

Post, S. 2003. A patent problem. *The Harvard Crimson,* https://www.thecrimson.com/article/2003/10/9/a-patent-problem-universities-like-harvard/.

Rawls, J. 1971. The Veil of Ignorance. A Theory of Justice, 136–141.

Ray, K. 2020. Black Bioethics and How the Failures of the Profession Paved the Way for Its Existence. *American Journal of Bioethics*. http://www.bioethics.net/2020/08/black-bioethics-and-how-the-failures-of-the-profession-paved-the-way-for-its-existence.

Richards, K., Hickey, K., & Ward, E. 2020. Drug pricing and pharmaceutical patenting practices. *Congressional Research Service*, https://sgp.fas.org/crs/misc/R46221.pdf.

Richardson, E., Malik, M, Darity, W., Mullen, A., Morse, M., Malif, M., Maybank, A., Bassett, M., Farmer, P., Worden, L., & Jones, J. 2021. Reparations for Black American descendants of persons enslaved in the US and their potential impact on SARS-CoV-2 transmission. *Social Science and Medicine* 276,113741. https://dx.doi.org/10.1016%2Fj.socscimed.2021.113741.

Robbins, R. 2021. Moderna, racing for profits, keeps COVID vaccine out of reach for poor. *The New York Times*. https://www.nytimes.com/2021/10/09/business/moderna-covid-vaccine.html?.

Roth, L., Bempong, D., Babigumira, J., Banoo, S., Cooke, E., Jeffreys, D., Kasonde, L., Leufkens, H., Lim, J., Lumpkin, M., Mahlangu, G., Peeling, R., Rees, H., Ndomondo-Sigonda, M., Stergachis, A., Ward, M., & Nwokike, J. 2018. Expanding global access to essential medicines: Investment priorities for sustainably strengthening medical product regulatory systems. *British Medical Journal* 14(102), https://doi.org/10.1186/s12992-018-0421-2.

Stout, J., & Leonard, E. 2018. Xtandi and the Activist perspective on access to medicines. *In APHA's 2018 Annual Meeting & Expo (Nov. 10–Nov. 14)*. APHA.

Trouillot, M. R. 1995. Silencing the Past: Power and the Production of History. Beacon Press Books.

UAEM Evidence. (n.d.). Universities Allied for Essential Medicine, Wordpress Blog. https://uaemevidence.wordpress.com.

Villarosa, L. 2018. Why America's black mothers and babies are in a life-or-death crisis. *The New York Times Magazine*, https://www.nytimes.com/2018/04/11/magazine/black-mothers-babies-death-maternal-mortality.html.

World Health Organization. 2004. *The World Medicines Situation*. Geneva, Switzerland. https://apps.who.int/iris/bitstream/handle/10665/68735/WHO_EDM_PAR_2004.5.pdf.

Yach, D., & Bettcher, D. 1998. The Globalization of Public Health, I: Threats and Opportunities. American Journal of Public Health 88(5), 735–738, https://dx.doi.org/10.2105%2Fajph.88.5.735.

Talking Foreign Policy Transcript

Talking Foreign Policy is a one-hour radio program, hosted by Case Western Reserve University School of Law Co-Dean Michael Scharf, in which experts discuss the salient foreign policy issues of the day. The quarterly broadcast is produced in partnership between Case Western Reserve University, the only US law school with its own foreign policy talk radio program, and WCPN 90.3 FM Ideastream, Cleveland's National Public Radio affiliate. Archived broadcasts are available for viewing in video format online at law.case.edu/TalkingForeignPolicy.

September 28, 2021, broadcast. *Blood & Treasure*[1]

Participants
Sandra Hodgkinson
Darin Johnson
Gregory P. Noone
Milena Sterio
Mark V. Vlasic

SCHARF: In the summer of 2019, CBS premiered *Blood & Treasure*,[2] a globe-trotting, action-adventure series about an intrepid international lawyer and a cunning art thief who team up to catch a ruthless terrorist. With 2.7 million viewers, the show was a hit, and it will be back for a second season in a few months. The exciting action drama was inspired by the real-life adventures of a group of international lawyers who hopscotch around the globe, working on war crimes prosecutions, human rights cases, and peace negotiations. They say that truth is sometimes more exciting than fiction. In this broadcast of WCPN's *Talking Foreign Policy*,[3] we will talk to four international lawyers whose actual adventures may have helped inspire the hit show, right after the news.

Who does not love a great action-adventure TV series? In the summer of 2019, millions tuned in to the show, *Blood & Treasure*, to see if a brilliant international lawyer and a cunning international art thief could stop a deadly terrorist. Two years earlier, my colleague, Mark Vlasic,[4] a former war crimes prosecutor and law professor, told me that he had pitched the idea for the show to CBS. "It is a story of international lawyer as action hero, a combination of Perry Mason and Indiana Jones," he told the studio. Not only did CBS greenlight the project, but it even hired Mark to serve as one of the executive producers. The show was a hit, and the second season will launch in a few months. Unfortunately, Mark could not join us today because he is on a plane to Europe. But, for this broadcast, I have assembled four international lawyers, all friends of Mark, whose real-life adventures may have helped inspire the series. Welcome to *Talking Foreign Policy.* I am your host, Michael Scharf, Dean of Case Western Reserve University School of Law.[5] In this broadcast, our panel of international lawyers will be sharing their real-life adventures on the four corners of the globe. We will hear about the challenges and the dangers that they encountered in their important work bringing war criminals to justice, stopping human rights violations, and negotiating peace agreements. Our guests today are all affiliated with the Public International Law and Policy Group (PILPG),[6] a non-governmental organization that I co-founded twenty-four years ago, and which was nominated for the Nobel Peace Prize. The group has provided legal counsel in fifteen peace negotiations. It has helped established a dozen international and domestic war crimes and piracy tribunals. Its members have testified before Congress, and its reports and briefs have been cited recently by the International Criminal Court. So, first, let me welcome Gregory ("Greg") Noone.[7] When you think Greg Noone, think Harmon Rabb, the lead character in the television series, *JAG.*[8] They even look a little bit alike. Well, he says he looks more like Tom Cruise. Greg is a retired JAG Captain[9] and former commanding officer of the Navy's International and Operational Law Unit. He is currently an Adjunct Professor at Case Western Reserve University School of Law, Director of the National Security and Intelligence Program at Fairmont State University and serves as the Executive Director of the Public International Law and Policy Group. Welcome to the show, Greg.

NOONE: Thank you, Mike. It is a pleasure to be here, and, just for the record, I am taller than Tom Cruise.

SCHARF: Next, it is my pleasure to introduce Sandra ("Sandy") Hodgkinson.[10] Sandy has served in high-level positions in the State Department and the Department of Defense, including as Deputy of the War Crimes Office at the State Department, Deputy Assistant Secretary of Defense for Detainee Affairs, and Senior Advisor of the Coalition Provisional Authority in Baghdad, Iraq. Sandy is currently Senior Vice President at Leonardo DRS, the subsidiary of the European-based Defense and Aerospace Conglomerate, and she is also a Senior Fellow at Public International Law and Policy Group. Welcome, Sandy.

HODGKINSON: Thanks so much, Michael. I am excited to be here today.

SCHARF: And I am also happy to introduce Darin Johnson,[11] Professor of Law at Howard University in Washington, DC. Darin served as Legal Advisor to the US Embassy in Iraq after the fall of Saddam Hussein, and then he was Chief of Staff for the Office of Special Coordinator of Middle East Transitions during the Arab Spring Uprisings.[12] Darin is also a Senior Legal Advisor at the Public International Law and Policy Group. Welcome, Darin.

JOHNSON: Thanks, Michael. Pleasure to be here.

SCHARF: Rounding out our panel of adventurers is Professor Milena Sterio,[13] who has been a regular on this show. Milena is a Chaired Professor at Cleveland State's Marshall College of Law, and she is the Managing Director of the Public International Law and Policy Group. It is so good to have you back.

STERIO: It is great to be back, Michael.

SCHARF: The television series, *Blood & Treasure*, is known for its exotic settings around the world. One of the best parts of being a real-life international lawyer is the travel. In my work, I have visited the temples of Angkor Wat, the ancient rock-cut cities of Petra, I have ridden on a stallion around the Great Pyramids of Giza, and I even white-water-rafted down the Nile near Lake Victoria. Let's turn to Greg Noone to tell us all about some of the exciting things he has done and seen in his work travels.

NOONE: Thank you, Michael. At risk of sounding like we are all trying to top each other with the amazing things that we have been able to experience. I know some of my colleagues, Sandy, in particular, has done some of the same things I have—truly, it has been remarkable. Sitting with the mountain gorillas in Rwanda, riding a camel in the Sahara at sunrise in Timbuktu, literally Timbuktu—definitely the first kid on my block to get there. Seeing tortoises that are 150 years old that were born during the American Civil War in Mauritius—just remarkable. More poignantly, being able to visit Nelson Mandela's cell on Robben Island[14] and standing in the Valley of Death in Crimea where the Light Brigade faithfully charged.[15] Lastly, witnessing the mothers of the disappeared protest in the

Plaza De Mayo in Buenos Aires.[16] It has really been a full range of exotic and poignant and important experiences.

SCHARF: Yeah, and the key is that you don't go on vacations. You might stick a vacation in at the end, but you are all there on someone else's dime doing international law work. Right, Greg?

NOONE: No, 100%. My dad always marveled at the fact that I was able to get someone else to pay for my world travels.

SCHARF: Darin, during your work in Rwanda, you got to see the Genocide Museum[17] and Hotel Rwanda.[18] Can you tell us about that experience?

JOHNSON: Yes, Michael. It was a really powerful experience. I was in Kigali, Rwanda, for one of PILPG's programs. We were essentially training a group of young African leaders from about ten different countries on transitional justice and how they could take these lessons in transitional justice back to their home countries that were experiencing ongoing civil conflict. What was so powerful about this experience was actually being there with these young, early-twenties leaders and hearing from Rwandans themselves about the genocide and about how they had worked to reconcile beyond those divisions. It was really powerful.

SCHARF: Darin, did Hotel Rwanda look a lot like it did in the movie?

JOHNSON: You know, it didn't, only because when we got to Hotel Rwanda, we were able to tour the outside, but we weren't able to go inside, so we weren't able to quite see it in the same way that it appeared in the film. But, by just being there and hearing the stories people had experienced, you still really felt like you were a part of that history.

SCHARF: Sandy, what is your favorite travel adventure?

HODGKINSON: Like my colleagues here, I have visited a lot of the war crimes sites and locations, both for pleasure and for work.

SCHARF: Only an international lawyer could say that they visited a war crimes site for pleasure.

HODGKINSON: Yes, but I have enjoyed some of the other sites, like some biblical sites, including Nineveh[19] and the Hanging Gardens of Babylon,[20] during my time in Iraq. I think a highlight for me in Lebanon was being able to go skiing at the Cedars.[21] I was provided a security detail for that ski trip, but, unfortunately, they had a lot of trouble keeping up, so I think I was actually at greater risk, because I had to keep stopping to wait for them on the slopes. It was truly a beautiful, remarkable place to visit.

SCHARF: Milena, what is yours?

STERIO: There are definitely several. One that comes to mind is when I spent six months in Baku, Azerbaijan, as a Fulbright Scholar. As part of our stay there, we got to see these oil platforms in the Caspian Sea that were featured in a James Bond movie some years before that. I would add to that visiting some of the ancient Roman ruins in Jordan where I was participating in a PILPG training program. We were training Yemeni lawyers, and I got to go around and see Petra,[22] but also some of the most memorable Roman ruins.

SCHARF: So, become an international lawyer, see the world. But the most rewarding aspect of being an international lawyer is the high-impact work that you all do. Let me ask each of our panelists to tell us about the most important project that they ever worked on. I'm going to begin with Sandy. Sandy, you were the Senior Advisor on Human Rights for the US Government in Iraq right after the fall of Saddam Hussein in 2003.[23] Tell us about your work there.

HODGKINSON: My time working with the Iraqi people was one of the highlights of my career. It was the most meaningful work that I got to participate in, and it really drove the direction of my career. I traveled over in the very beginning of the conflict just prior to staying with General Jay Garner and his team in Kuwait, and we came in right when Saddam Hussein fell and helped establish the new Iraqi government there. My role in all of that was really to help drive a culture of human rights and to address the atrocities that had occurred under the prior regime of Saddam Hussein. When I first came in, I got to start working with local NGOs on the ground establishing new culture for human rights and a human rights ministry as a part of the new government. As time went on, I was also able to work with them on establishing mechanisms for accountability for the atrocities under Saddam's regime. That was extremely meaningful because they were seeking a domestic tribunal under Iraqi law to try him for his war crimes. I got the opportunity to work with the new Iraqi government on helping set that up and see the process through the collection of evidence and the ultimate preparation for trial. This was a highlight of my career—getting to work with them, help them move beyond what they had suffered, and try to create a country that respected fundamental rights, human rights, and human rights law.

SCHARF: I am going to turn next to Greg, who recently led PIGLP's team that documented the Rohingya genocide[24] by interviewing over

1,000 survivors in Cox's Bazar, Bangladesh. Greg, can you tell us about that experience?

NOONE: It was an amazing experience. We had a tremendous team. We went into the refugee camps and undertook this survey of random interviews. Basically, the Rohingya, chased out of their home country, Myanmar—or Burma, as many may know it—suffered at the hands of not only the national military, but also some militias and other people joining in. It was one of the most depraved stories I had ever heard. Forgive me for sounding like a bit of a sociopath, but I was used to hearing: "They surrounded the village. They killed some men. They raped some women, and they burned down the village." But they went to the next level. They were dismembering people. They were taking babies out of the arms of mothers and throwing them into the fire or throwing them into the river. In one horrific story, they made one man select which woman would be raped by all the soldiers in front of the rest of the village. It was really a level of depravity that shakes you to your core, but, ultimately, by collecting this, you are able to let the world know what happened there.

SCHARF: Being an international lawyer is not for the faint of heart. It is time for a short station break. When we return, we are going to talk about some of the things that went wrong during the panelists' work in some of the most dangerous parts of the globe. Stay with us.

SCHARF: Welcome back to *Talking Foreign Policy*, brought to you by Case Western Reserve University and WCPN 90.3 Ideastream. I am Michael Scharf, Dean of Case Western Reserve University School of Law. I am talking today with four international lawyers whose adventures around the globe may have helped inspire the hit television series, *Blood & Treasure*, produced by our friend, Mark Vlasic. We are getting to the most interesting part of the discussion: times when things did not quite go as expected. In every good action adventure, there is always a moment when everything goes wrong. So it is in real life. Let me begin with Darin Johnson. Darin is legal advisor to the US Embassy in Iraq. You literally landed in Baghdad the day Saddam Hussein was executed. Instead of a somber affair, cellphone video captured the guards mocking Saddam and celebrating as he was led to the gallows. A few minutes later, when Saddam's brother, Barzan, was hanged, his head was torn from his body.[25] You have told me that your first assignment in Iraq was damage control regarding these botched executions. Can you tell us about that?

JOHNSON: Yeah, absolutely Michael. It was a memorable moment, to say the least. I was a young State Department lawyer. This was my first overseas assignment, and I landed in the country to this major crisis. Sandy had mentioned before, the effort to stand up this domestic tribunal was with the goal of bringing about justice for Saddam's crimes. This botched execution, and with it being recorded, really undermined that effort and risked turning the whole tribunal into this caricature of retribution, so, behind the scenes, we had a lot of negotiation and discussions with the Iraqi government to pause their implementation of the death penalty, to make sure that the procedures were in place to ensure that there was no recording of any further executions, and, certainly, to ensure that, to the extent that they were carrying out executions, that they were carried out in a manner that was not as horrendous as the instance with Barzan. It was definitely trial by fire for a young international lawyer and definitely a memorable moment.

SCHARF: Next, let me turn to Sandy Hodgkinson. Sandy, when you were Deputy Assistant Secretary of Defense for Detainee Affairs during the Bush Administration, you managed to all but empty the notorious Guantanamo Bay detention center by convincing countries to take custody of their citizen detainees. Instead of celebrating your successes, you were called to Congress to testify when some of the repatriated detainees returned to the battlefield and attacked US personnel. What was that like for you?

HODGKINSON: Well, a key lesson here is that the decision-making process on international law and policy matters is very complex and multifaceted. As a result, it can get very emotional when different perspectives are brought to the table. Here, we needed to balance the need to protect against these very dangerous individuals that had been encountered on the battlefield and the stronger desire to close Guantanamo at the same time. In trying to balance those, we carefully constructed a situation where we would negotiate with host countries for the transfer of individuals from Guantanamo back to their home countries, only provided that they gave us assurances that those individuals would not be able to come back and fight us in the future. But, in not every circumstance did the countries honor those promises, so in the balance of trying to close down the numbers at Guantanamo Bay, we had to trust our allies and our partners in trying to reach that goal. People fell on different sides of the debate as to whether or not you should continue to detain these individuals at Guantanamo Bay or whether you should try to close Guantanamo. Here is a clear example of the real challenge between balancing that need for security and safety and trying to do the right thing.

SCHARF: International law and diplomacy is full of stories of unintended consequences. Milena Sterio, while you were assisting with piracy prosecutions in the Seychelles and Mauritius, you learned that the Western approach known as "catch and release"[26] had the unintended consequences of encouraging the recruitment and use of children as pirates. You were then invited to speak about the challenges of combating child piracy at the UN Working Group in Copenhagen.[27] What was your advice to the UN, and what did we learn from that?

STERIO: Michael, you and I had the privilege of working with prosecutors and judges in the Seychelles and Mauritius, and they told us that if they had suspect detainees who were under the age of eighteen, their first reflex was just to say, "We are going to stay away from this. This is just too complicated. We do not want to prosecute them." When we spoke to the UN, our advice was that it was crucial not to have a "catch and release" policy when it comes to juvenile piracy suspects. Instead, it was key to train those judges and prosecutors on appropriate international human rights standards that apply to the detention and prosecution of juvenile suspects. Under international human rights law, juveniles can be prosecuted, but they have to be detained in separate facilities, they have to be provided with educational opportunities, and their sentences should reflect their young age.[28]

SCHARF: Did you also recommend that when adult pirates were being prosecuted, it should be an aggravating factor in sentencing if they went out to sea with children?

STERIO: Absolutely. At the beginning of some of these prosecutions, there was a tendency to prosecute the entire group of piracy suspects together, including juveniles and the ringleaders. Our advice there was to say, "No. No. No. That's not right." The ringleaders should actually receive harsher penalties because they recruited and used child pirates.[29]

SCHARF: We were talking about Milena's experience in the Seychelle Islands and Mauritius, which are both in the Indian ocean. In *Blood & Treasure*, the TV series, our protagonists stay at luxurious hotels and beautiful cities. It is not all about tents and sleeping bags for real-life international lawyers either. Milena, tell us about your accommodations and the amenities in Mauritius.

STERIO: Sure, Michael. I definitely have stayed in places that were not so nice, but, in Mauritius, it was literally the opposite. We stayed at a luxurious resort with lots of water sports, a spa, a wonderful restaurant. To be totally honest, it was nice after a full day of work talking about human rights standards and children. It was nice to go back to this luxurious hotel and unwind.

SCHARF: Best advertisement ever for going to law school.

STERIO: Yes.

SCHARF: Let's contrast that experience with the experience that Greg and Sandy had in Côte d'Ivoire. You guys are not going to believe some of this. Go ahead. Who wants to start, Greg or Sandy?

NOONE: First, I would just say that we were there after the electoral violence and working on transitional justice. Sandy and I were flying around the country, compliments of the UN. This one particular hotel looked like it was right out of the *Pirates of the Caribbean* ride at Disney World. The night that we stayed there, it rained like I have never seen rain ever before. This rain just absolutely deluged for four straight hours. It was amazing. My room was in the lee of the building. There was this beautiful misting rain coming in. "Africa," the song, was going through my head. On the other hand, Sandy, what was your experience in that same hotel?

HODGKINSON: I do recall that Greg woke up all refreshed the next morning bragging about the great night sleep he had, while I was actually up all night long because it was so creaky, I was scared. It was also partly because we had a meal just before we went into the hotel. At the only place that they had where you could eat, you would watch them take the plate of the customer before you, dunk it in a bucket of brown, murky water, and then put your chicken on it and hand it to you. After our fine meal, we did go back to our *Pirates of the Caribbean* hotel. It was truly frightening.

NOONE: I will just say this, Michael. The roof was like a corrugated tin roof that sounded like it was going to blow off, so what Sandy is leaving out is that she put her running sneakers on and was ready to launch at any given minute when the roof finally blew off, whereas I did get a wonderful night's sleep.

SCHARF: I think she mentioned to me that she literally slept standing up that night. Is that right, Sandy?

HODGKINSON: Absolutely.

SCHARF: Sometimes the situation outside the premises is so dire that international lawyers have to be locked down inside for their safety. Darin, tell us about your experience during the Juba peace negotiations in 2019–2020.[30]

JOHNSON: Absolutely, Michael. As part of PILPG's delegation, I was one of the lawyers supporting the negotiations between different Sudanese parties, which South Sudan was hosting. Even though South Sudan was hosting these peace negotiations for its neighbor, South Sudan itself was also in the midst of its own very active and very violent civil conflict. As we traveled into the country, we had our own security, and we were under a very tight curfew. At one point during the negotiations, we were actually locked down in our compound because there was very actionable intelligence that surfaced that terrorist groups were about to target expat sites. Essentially all of the locations where expatriots and international lawyers, such as ourselves, were staying were subject to attack. Fortunately, our team took it very seriously. We were locked down for a period of time, but, once we moved past that period, we were back at it.

STERIO: Michael, if I can jump in, I know that you yourself have been in the thick of things several times. Tell us about the time that you were threatened by child soldiers at a checkpoint in Libya.

SCHARF: That is a good one. We were in Libya to do transitional justice work and we decided to go to Misrata, which was the height of the greatest fighting during the Libyan Civil War.[31] On the way there, there was a checkpoint manned by a child soldier who had machine guns wrapped around his neck. He stopped the car in front of us, made the passenger-seat passenger get out, and started bashing him with his machine guns. Then, he let him get back in the car and waived him forward. Then, we pulled up, and I was sitting in the passenger seat. He started yelling for me to get out. I looked pleadingly at the driver to do something. He started speaking in Arabic, and the child soldier started speaking back, and then he looked very disappointed and waived us forward. I said to the driver, "What in the world did you do? You're a miracle worker." And, he says, "Oh no, you are just really lucky, professor. I happen to know his dad, and I told him that, if he beat you up, I was going to tell on him." I dodged the bullet on that one. But, yeah, you are right. Sometimes, things can get really hairy in the field.

STERIO: You definitely lucked out on that one. What about the time that you got tear gassed in Istanbul?

SCHARF: I did not miss the bullet that time. We were there training and working with Syrian judges for the future prosecution of the Assad regime. That happened to be the day that college kids did a mass protest in Taksim Square in Istanbul.[32] We were about a mile away at a Starbucks talking with these Syrian judges, and all of a sudden, we heard chanting and yelling, and a flood of people came into our square. They were the people who had been protesting in Taksim. They were subject to tear gassing, and rubber bullets, and water cannons. The next thing I know, we were subject to all of that. We started running with the protestors, like one might run with the bulls at Pamplona.[33] I never ran so fast in my whole life. We ended up peeling off and making it back to the hotel. The next day we met with the Syrian judges and said, "Where did you guys go? We lost track of you." They said, "Oh, when you ran away, professor, we ran toward the riot police. We picked up the tear gas and threw it back at them." I said, "That is kind of dangerous. Why would you do that?" They said, "Because, in our own country, Syria, when we protest, we get shot at with real bullets, they drop barrel bombs on us, and they use chlorine gas against us. Tear gas is nothing. This was part of democracy." That was their way of celebrating democracy very heroically.

STERIO: I guess all is relative, right?

SCHARF: You know, we were talking earlier about exotic travel, but you all have seen some horrible things too during your work excursions. Greg, tell us about your experience when you visited the massacre sites in Rwanda just after the 1994 genocide.[34]

NOONE: It was really something. I was part of a team that was training the thirty-nine surviving prosecutors so that they could do the best to prosecute the genocide. There was already talk about how not that many people were killed—and did it really happen—almost on the level of a Holocaust denial. At this one particular site where about 3,000 people were killed—it was at a school—they exhumed all of the bodies that had been shoved into a pit. Then, they laid all the bodies out in the school rooms, the classrooms, and covered them in lime. On the door, they wrote the number of bodies that were in each room, and they brought us there because they wanted internationals to see this with their own eyes so that they could do the math, look at these 3,000 exhumed bodies, know how big the village was, and kind of extrapolate to get to 800,000. I can tell you that I will never get the smell of lime out of my nose. I can still smell it today.

SCHARF: I am convinced that Milena gets all of the really good excursions, and Greg gets the really difficult ones. Sandy, what were the most difficult things that you saw during your work?

HODGKINSON: Perhaps, the most heart-wrenching experience that I had was not dissimilar to what Greg just described. This was immediately after the fall of Saddam Hussein, when local communities down in the Hillah central area of Iraq, just South of Baghdad, began digging up all of the mass graves there looking for their loved ones who had gone missing under his regime, and, most specifically, in the 1991 Shia uprising.[35] They had all come out and were looking for all of their loved ones. There were mothers, grandmothers, parents, fathers, brothers, sisters, all just digging up the earth with their bare hands, wailing and crying, and looking for any item to help identify their loved ones—a piece of clothing, a personal effect, or something so that they could have a confirmation that they were, in fact, deceased and, also, to offer them a proper burial. Like Greg, the memory of that will stay with me forever, as they tried to reconcile that and we tried to offer our assistance to get them through that process.

SCHARF: That really is heart-wrenching. Darin, what about you?

JOHNSON: I would say that the most heart-wrenching experience was, again, when I was serving in Baghdad. There was an incident where contractors ended up killing over a dozen civilians in Nisour Square.[36] I was part of a team of embassy officials responsible for meeting with the family members. I just remember spending days sitting in a tent meeting with family members and discussing what had happened. It was probably one of the most personally heart-wrenching experiences that I have gone through.

SCHARF: Darin, you also helped advise Iraqi human rights defenders documenting the abuses of ISIS. Can you tell us about that?

JOHNSON: Absolutely, Michael. Not long after ISIS was defeated in large part in Iraq, PILPG was able to return to the country. We had not been able to get into the country for a quite some time because of the conflict. We worked with this coalition of human rights defenders from around the country who had taken up the responsibility of documenting the abuses of ISIS to try to bring some accountability and some reparation to family members who had been impacted by it. It was really difficult work, but really heroic Iraqi citizens engaged in that effort.

SCHARF: It is time for another short break. When we return, I am going to ask our experts about times when cultural differences led to "lost in translation" type of situations. We will be back in just a minute.

SCHARF: This is Michael Scharf, and we are back with *Talking Foreign Policy*. I am joined today by four international lawyers whose adventures may have helped inspire the television series, *Blood & Treasure*. In this final segment, we are going to talk about times when things went wrong because of cultural misunderstandings.

STERIO: Michael, why don't you kick us off by telling the story that appears in your book, *Enemy of the State*,[37] about when you were about to tell the Iraqi judges that they should be like a pit bull about due process?

SCHARF: That is a good one. I learned a lesson there. I was invited to help train the judges for the Saddam Hussein trial,[38] and I was trying to convince them that they had to be really vigilant about due process because the whole world was watching them.[39] So, I said, "You have to be like a pit bull when it comes to due process and fair trial rights." My interpreter said, "What is a pit bull?" I said, "A pit bull is this dog we have in the United States that bites the neck and will not let go." I said that they needed to be like that about due process. He said, "No, professor, I will not say that about the pit bull." I said, "Why?" He said, "Because, in our country, the dog is a very evil creature. It is a dirty creature, and to even suggest that the judges must be like a dog, well, they would walk out of the room and never talk to you again." So, I said, "Well, do you guys have tree frogs in those marsh Arab areas? You know, sticky frogs that will not let go?" He says, "Oh, we have many sticky frogs, professor." I said, "Well, tell them they have to be like a sticky frog then." It was not quite the same analogy or metaphor, but it worked, and they did not leave the room. Milena, speaking of interpreters, why don't you tell us about what the interpreter said to you when you were in Amman, Jordan, working with lawyers from Yemen as part of the peace negotiations?

STERIO: Sure. I was in Amman, Jordan, as part of this Public International Law and Policy Group peace negotiation that lasted for about five days, and it was in English and Arabic.[40] Most of the Yemeni lawyers did not speak English and were speaking Arabic, so there were interpreters there interpreting from English to Arabic and the other way around. At the end of the first day, one of the interpreters came up to me very seriously and said, "You know, we interpreters, we keep a hit list." I looked at him, and I said, "What do you mean?" He said, "A hit list of people who speak too fast." He said, "And, right now, you are number one on that list." That was a good way of reminding me to slow down because the interpreters were having a really hard time.

SCHARF: Whenever I speak at a conference with simultaneous interpretation, I always have a sign sitting in front of me at the dais that says "slow down," for that reason. Sandy, being a woman in the field can have unique challenges in some foreign countries, and you once told me that, in Botswana, the local colonel that you were working with asked you if he could call you "mama." Is that right? What did you say to him?

HODGKINSON: I told him that "lieutenant" would be just fine.

SCHARF: Are there other times when you ran into such gender challenges?

HODGKINSON: As a female officer, beginning in the military in uniform and then separately as a diplomat when I worked for the State Department, I had a number of interesting encounters, not really challenges but just interesting moments where we were trying to understand the awkwardness and how to handle a female and male relationship in a foreign country. I felt like I was considered this sort of third gender because I had been placed in a position of authority by the US government. I was not really male, but I was not a local female by their standards. I was sort of a different thing. It seemed like I was this third gender, and they would allow me to be assertive in my positions and still earn respect. It calls up a few memories that I had that were really special, though. One was in Mauritania when I was there as the senior member of a delegation and was invited to a dinner at the local colonel's home. I was the only female seated around this incredible display of food, but it was all being served by the daughters and spouse of the colonel. They kept peering out from the kitchen to watch me and giggling all night long because they could not believe that there was actually a woman there. I compare that to a time when I did a three-week peacekeeping trip in Abu Dhabi, and, every night, the male officers were invited to go out with members of the Emirati Armed Forces for dinners and events. As a female, I was separately paired up with a different spouse for every night of the trip and would go to local markets to go shopping or have tea but was kept completely by myself one spouse at a time. I got to share so many stories about our cultural differences. I think I will only mention one more because I, to this day, still think about this with such fondness. I was visiting Beirut just prior to getting married, and the admiral there had heard about my engagement and threw this big engagement party for me at the officer's club. All of the male officers that I had worked with over the years each individually gave me a beautiful gift, which was a makeup kit. I ended up stuffing my suitcase, coming home with like fifty-five different kinds of eye shadows and lipsticks and perfumes to bring back for me to get married with. It was extremely endearing, and I cherish some of those memories. But I was a different thing than what they were used to.

SCHARF: I do want to point out that Sandy now has five wonderful children and, for the record, they are the only ones who get to call her "mama." Now, phrases in different cultures sometimes mean something very different than their literal translation. Darin, did you ever experience that in your work in the Middle East?

JOHNSON: Definitely, Michael. One kind of funny moment that I remember is when I served as legal advisor for our embassy in Baghdad. One of my jobs was to regularly meet with high-level Iraqi officials and, oftentimes, when I would make a request of them or I had to deliver a particular message from the State Department, I would receive a response of "in sha'Allah" or "God willing." That usually sounded like a pretty positive response until I found out from some close Iraqi friends that I made that, oftentimes, "in sha'Allah" is just another way of saying "don't bet on it." That moment showed me the importance of having friends who are local who can tell you what the terms really mean.

SCHARF: I think I just learned something. You know, in different cultures there are different conceptions of being on time. I know in US sports there is a saying that if you are early, you are on time, if you are on time, you are late, and, if you are late, you better be running laps. But it is quite different abroad. To illustrate this, Milena, why don't you tell us about the time you had a 10:00 meeting with the Dean of Novi Sad Law School in Serbia and showed up a couple of minutes early?

STERIO: Yeah. I showed up at around 9:55, thinking, I am early. I am not running laps. I am early. When I showed up and checked in with the dean's secretary, she looked at me as if I were completely crazy. I said, "No, I am here for the 10:00 meeting." She said, "Yeah, but it is 9:57." I said, "Yeah..."

She said, "You know he is not going to be available" or "It does not really start until 10:30 or 10:40." There was a totally different conception of time. I am sure Darin would agree with this, for example, in Juba, South Sudan, where both of us spent time for peace negotiations. After a few days there, my Western colleagues and I started saying things like, "Oh, does this really start at 10:00 a.m. normal time, or 10:00 a.m. Juba time?"

SCHARF: Yeah, and food can be a big challenge, too. Monkey brains in parts of Africa, snake soup in China, sheep's head in Norway, fat-bottomed ants in Colombia, guinea pigs in Peru, crocodile skewers in Australia—they are all foreign delicacies that have been offered to me while I have been working abroad. I remember once when I was in Libya, we had just finished a large midday feast with our host, and my colleague, Paul Williams, who has often been on the show, asked the question, "What does camel taste like?" On our way back to the office after this feast, our host took a detour for a second lunch at a restaurant with a large camel sign out front. But sometimes the shoe is on the other foot, and we have to remember that what we eat in the United States might seem a little odd to our foreign guests. Greg, tell us the story about the time you hosted a Rwandan delegation in Newport, Rhode Island.

NOONE: Yeah, thanks Michael. So, each night we would take turns bringing them out to dinner, and Newport, Rhode Island, of course, has wonderful restaurants. The night before my turn, one of our colleagues did a classic New England clambake. You can imagine the whole scene that they put on for them. I thought, how wonderful. I always love to go to a New England clambake. The next night, I was taking them out, and I said, "Where would you like to eat?" They kind of sheepishly looked around each other and finally said, "Anything, but no more giant red scorpion."

SCHARF: That is what our lobsters are to them?

NOONE: Yeah, it took me a minute to realize that they were talking about lobsters, and then I thought, if I was in the middle of Africa and somebody put a big beetle on my plate and said, "This a delicacy. This costs a lot of money, and, here, eat the back end first," I think would have the same reaction, so, yes, sometimes we miss the boat as well.

STERIO: Now, Michael, tell us the story about your meeting with the Head of the Truth Commission in Côte D'Ivoire.[41]

SCHARF: Oh yeah, Côte D'Ivoire, the same place where Sandy and Greg were at the hotel in the rain. I went there at the behest of the US

State Department to talk to the Head of the Truth Commission, who had reportedly decided that she was going to release the names of everybody who had been implicated or who had testified before her commission, whether or not there was any corroboration or any evidence that showed that these people were implicated beyond a reasonable doubt. The problem, of course, is that once you are named in a Truth Commission report, it is like putting a target on you, and people are going to attack you. I had this very important assignment to go and convince her to keep those names secret, give them only to the prosecutor, and have an executive summary without the names. I go there, and I do not speak really good French. In Côte d'Ivoire, that is all that they speak. I know Sandy speaks French really well and Milena is fluent in French, but not Greg and me, right Greg? When I was there, I said that I would be using a translator and, all of a sudden, the Truth Commission Judge got very angry and started saying a lot of things in rapid French. I heard her say, "Newt Gingrich" and "Mitt Romney." This was very perplexing to me, so I turned to the translator and said, "What's going on?" Apparently, this was during the primaries when Newt Gingrich and Mitt Romney were running against each other, and Newt Gingrich had a commercial that aired everywhere in the world, through the beauty of computers, in which he showed Mitt Romney speak in French at the Salt Lake City Olympics.[42] Newt Gingrich's voice-over said, "That is Mitt Romney, and he speaks French too well to be a patriot. Someone who speaks French that well is unfit to be president. Vote Newt Gingrich." That made this French-speaking judge very angry, so I had to find a way to extract myself from that. I noticed that she had some pictures of her kids playing soccer on her desk, so I started asking her questions about her kids to distract her. Then, I asked her if the kids knew about the important work that their mom was doing, and I said, "Because you know if you do not end up documenting these atrocities, your country is going to be condemned to repeat them over and over again." Now, of course, I was shamelessly borrowing from George Santayana,[43] but she did not seem to know that. She thought that was pretty cool, so she asked if she could have her selfie taken with me, and we worked things out. But, yes, it is very important as an international lawyer sometimes to be able to speak the local language. I want to end by asking each of our panelists why they became international lawyers. I will start with you, Milena.

STERIO: Sure. For me, maybe it is a little bit personal. I grew up in what is now Serbia, the former Yugoslavia. When I was coming of age, the country was falling apart. There was a civil war, and lots of bad things were happening. I really saw first-hand the role that international lawyers can play in resolving conflicts and leading the parties towards an agreement. From that point on, I decided that this was what I would like to be. This is what I would like to do and, hopefully, I will someday make an impact in either my own country or somewhere else.

SCHARF: You certainly have. Darin, you are next.

JOHNSON: Similar to Milena, I grew up with a deep reverence for the role that lawyers can play in improving society. I grew up with this deep reverence for civil rights lawyers, and I also had a passion for foreign affairs. I found that, over time, a career in international law really allowed me to merge all of those passions: a deep love of the law, a deep love of foreign affairs, and a deep love of human rights. It has been so, so rewarding.

SCHARF: Greg, how about you?

NOONE: Well, I wish it was as deep as Darin's. I was a young, single naval officer who just wanted to be stationed overseas. I kind of fell into it quite by accident and then came back to Newport, Rhode Island, and worked at a brand-new program called the Defense Institute of International Legal Studies,[44] which is a place where Sandy and I both worked. We got to do some amazing work from all over the world and really fell in love with the idea that we could practice law, help others practice law, and, along the way, help victims of some of the gravest atrocities known to man.

SCHARF: Sandy, what about you?

HODGKINSON: I always had this passion for human rights and international law, even before there were classes in this area. As I was going through school, I was always interested in and fascinated by the war crimes tribunals and how to address them. Long before there was an International Criminal Court, I authored a big paper on why we should have an International Criminal Court because I felt so strongly that there had to be justice mechanisms for accountability. Through this opportunity to serve in this capacity as a lawyer over these decades, it has been everything I ever hoped it could be and more. I have loved every step of the career.

SCHARF: Finally, with a few minutes remaining, I would love to ask each of you to tell us about what you are working on now and where you are going to be traveling next. Milena, do you want to kick things off?

STERIO: Sure. Lately, I have been very involved in the work of the Public International Law and Policy Group. I just returned from a round of peace negotiations in Juba, South Sudan, so it is likely that I will return to Juba. We also have a potential visit scheduled in Khartoum, Sudan, where we work with the government of Sudan, and then we also have clients in Ukraine. Those are the destinations that are most likely in the near future.

SCHARF: Darin, what about you?

JOHNSON: Much like Milena, I have worked with PILPG on the Sudan peace negotiations. Right now, I am working on a team helping to focus on implementation of that agreement. I am also working on human rights documentation in Iraq and transitional justice in South Sudan. Hopefully, there will be opportunities to travel back to Juba, both in support of the Sudan peace negotiations and transitional justice issues in South Sudan.

SCHARF: Greg, where are you off to next?

NOONE: I literally just returned from Amman, Jordan, where we are helping the Jordanian Armed Forces create operational legal support. Basically, we are making international lawyers out of some of their military lawyers so that they can better advise commanders in the field, especially with their treatment of civilians, whether refugees or people caught in between battle. I am also working with the Public International Law and Policy Group to lead the Yemen team. As you can imagine, there is never a dull moment when working with Yemen.

SCHARF: We have heard some fascinating tales from the field today. Do not be surprised if some of these show up in the next season of *Blood & Treasure.* Our producer is indicating that it is time to wrap up our program. Greg Noone, Sandy Hodgkinson, Darin Johnson, and Milena Sterio, thank you all for sharing your experiences with our listeners. Our audience will probably never think about international lawyers in the same way again. I am Michael Scharf. You have been listening to *Talking Foreign Policy.*

Notes

1. Transcribed by Case Western Reserve School of Law's Senior Cox Center International Law Fellow, Sydney Warinner, and Cox Center International Law Fellows, Alyse Geiger, Jose Mendez, and Dana Tysyachuk.

2. *See 7 Cool Things We Learned About Blood & Treasure,* CBS, https://www.cbs.com/shows/watch_magazine/photos/1008735/7-cool-things-we-learned-about-blood-treasure/ (last visited Nov. 24, 2021).

3. *Talking Foreign Policy*, Case Western Reserve University School of Law, https://case.edu/law/centers-institutes/cox-international-law-center/talking-foreign-policy (last visited

Nov. 24, 2021). *Talking Foreign Policy* is a radio program hosted by Michael Scharf that discusses current foreign policy issues. Case Western Reserve University School of Law, in partnership with WCPN, produces the show.
4. Mark V. Vlasic, Georgetown Law, https://www.law.georgetown.edu/faculty/mark-vlasic/ (last visited Nov. 24, 2021). Mark Vlasic is a Senior Fellow and Adjunct Professor of Law at Georgetown University and previously worked for the White House, the Pentagon, the World Bank, and the United Nations.
5. Michael P. Scharf, JD, Case Western Reserve University School of Law, https://case.edu/law/our-school/faculty-directory/michael-p-scharf (last visited Nov. 24, 2021). Michael Scharf is Co-Dean of Case Western Reserve University School of Law. He has written and published extensively in the area of international law.
6. See "A Global Pro Bono Law Firm," Public International Law and Policy Group, https://www.publicinternationallawandpolicygroup.org/ (last visited Nov. 24, 2021). PILPG is a global pro bono law firm that provides free legal services for peace negotiations and post-conflict, war-crimes prosecution, and transitional justice issues.
7. Dr. Gregory P. Noone, Public International Law and Policy Group, https://www.publicinternationallawandpolicygroup.org/dr-gregory-p-noone-bio (last visited Oct. 4, 2021). Gregory Noone is a Senior Peace Fellow and Senior Legal Advisor for the Public International Law and Policy Group. He is also an adjunct professor at Case Western Reserve University School of Law.
8. *JAG*, IMBD, https://www.imdb.com/title/tt0112022/(last visited Nov. 24, 2021). *JAG* follows the cases of Harmon Rabb and other lawyers in the US Navy's Judge Advocate General's office.
9. "About Navy JAG," US Navy Judge Advocate General's Corps, https://www.jag.navy.mil/about.htm (last visited Nov. 24, 2021). JAG provides legal counsel to commanders, sailors, and navy families to enable effective operations. JAG's core practice areas include military justice, operational law, and command advice.
10. Sandra Hodgkinson, Leonardo DRS, https://www.leonardodrs.com/who-we-are/our-leadership/sandra-l-hodgkinson/ (last visited Nov. 24, 2021). Sandra Hodgkinson is Senior Vice President at Leonardo DRS. She previously worked for the United States Department of Defense, the United States State Department, and the White House.
11. *See* Darin Johnson, HeinOnline, https://heinonline.org/HOL/AuthorProfile?base=js&search_name=Johnson,%20Darin&1==1601158823 (last visited Nov. 24, 2021). Darin Johnson is an Assistant Professor of Law at Howard University School of Law.
12. *See* Kali Robinson, *The Arab Spring at Ten Years: What's the Legacy of the Uprisings?*, Council on Foreign Relations (Dec. 3, 2020, 9:00 a.m. EST), https://www.cfr.org/article/arab-spring-ten-years-whats-legacy-uprisings. The Arab Spring Uprisings were incited by the protest of Mohamed Bouazizi and culminated in a revolutionary movement across the Middle East and North Africa, resulting in the toppling of several authoritarian regimes.
13. Milena Sterio, Cleveland-Marshall College of Law, https://www.law.csuohio.edu/meetcmlaw/faculty/sterio (last visited Nov. 24, 2021). Milena Sterio is a chaired professor at Cleveland-Marshall College of Law and an expert in international law.
14. *See* "27 May 1963: Mandela Arrives on Robben Island," Nelson Mandela Foundation, https://www.nelsonmandela.org/news/entry/27-may-1962-mandela-arrives-on-robben-island (last visited Dec. 16, 2021).
15. *See* Jesse Greenspan, *The Charge of the Light Brigade, 160 Years Ago*, History, https://www.history.com/news/the-charge-of-the-light-brigade-160-years-ago (updated Oct. 28, 2019). The Charge of the Light Brigade was a failed British cavalry charge against Russian troops during the Crimean War. The tragic event was memorialized in a famous poem by Alfred, Lord Tennyson in 1855.
16. *See* Erin Blakemore, *30,000 Were 'Disappeared' in Argentina's Dirty War. These Women Never Stopped Looking*, History (Mar. 7, 2019), https://www.history.com/news/mothers-plaza-de-mayo-disappeared-children-dirty-war-argentina.

17. "Kigali Genocide Memorial,"Visit Rwanda, https://www.visitrwanda.com/interests/kigali-genocide-memorial/ (last visited Oct. 4, 2021). The Kigali Genocide Memorial is the resting place for over 250,000 Tutsi victims in the Rwandan Genocide. This memorial is the largest, and several other smaller memorials are spread throughout the country.
18. *See* "Mille Collines," Genocide Archive of Rwanda, https://genocidearchiverwanda.org.rw/index.php/Category:Mille_Collines (last visited Oct. 4, 2021). *Hotel Rwanda* (or the Hôtel des Mille Collines) is a film depicting the hotel and its manager, Paul Rusesabagina, during the Rwandan Genocide. Rusesabagina and the hotel gained fame for taking in thousands of refugees in 1994.
19. *See* Joshua J. Mark, *Nineveh*, World History Encyclopedia (Mar. 06, 2011), https://www.worldhistory.org/nineveh/. Nineveh is a great city in antiquity. Now known Mosul, Iraq, Nineveh was a large, affluent trade center and is mentioned in the Bible. The city was destroyed in 612 BCE.
20. "Hanging Gardens of Babylon," United Nations Museum, http://www.unmuseum.org/mob/hangg.htm (last visited Oct. 4, 2021). The Hanging Gardens of Babylon were one of the Seven Wonders of the Ancient World.
21. "Cedars: Overview," Skileb, https://www.skileb.com/ski-resort/Cedars/ (last visited Oct. 4, 2021). The Cedars Ski Resort is in northern Lebanon. The Cedars is an ancient forest and has been open to skiers since 1920.
22. *The Ancient City of Petra*, American Museum of Natural History, https://www.amnh.org/explore/ology/archaeology/the-ancient-city-of-petra2 (last visited Oct. 4, 2021). The Ancient City of Petra was founded over 2,000 years ago. The city is comprised of elaborate buildings that are carved into the sandstone cliffs in the desert along a trade route in what is now the country of Jordan.
23. *See* "Saddam Hussein Fast Facts," CNN, https://www.cnn.com/2013/10/17/world/meast/saddam-hussein-fast-facts/index.html (Apr. 27, 2017, 3:42 p.m.).
24. "Rohingya," Human rights watch, https://www.hrw.org/tag/rohingya (last visited Oct. 18, 2021). The Rohingya people have faced decades of persecution by Myanmar governments. Approximately 900,000 Rohingya have relocated to camps in Bangladesh while another 600,000 remain in Rakhine State and still face persecution today.
25. John F. Burns, *Second Iraq Hanging Also Went Awry*, N.Y. Times, (Jan. 16, 2007), https://www.nytimes.com/2007/01/16/world/middleeast/16hang.html.
26. Mark A. Drumbl, *Child Pirates: Rehabilitation, Reintegration, and Accountability*, 46 Case W. Res. J. Int'l L. 235, 261 (2013) (discussing the usual practice of "catch and release," where naval forces capture juvenile pirates, confiscate their weapons, and immediately release them afterwards).
27. "Working Group on Children and Armed Conflict," United Nations, https://www.un.org/securitycouncil/subsidiary/wgcaac (last visited Oct. 4, 2021).
28. Convention on the Rights of the Child, art. 37(a), 37(c), 40(3)(b), Nov. 20, 1989, 1577 U.N.T.S. 3.
29. Milena Sterio, *Juvenile Pirates: "Lost Boys" or Violent Criminals?*, 46 Case W. Res. J. Int'l L. 279, 300 (2013) (discussing the recommendation of giving harsher penalties to those who employ juveniles in piracy).
30. *See* "Sudan's Government, Rebel Groups Sign Landmark Deal," Al Jazeera (Oct. 3, 2020), https://www.aljazeera.com/news/2020/10/3/sudans-government-rebels-set-to-sign-landmak-deal; Juba Agreement for Peace in Sudan Between the Transitional Government of Sudan and Parties to Peace Process, Oct. 3, 2020, https://www.peaceagreements.org/viewmasterdocument/2325.
31. Portia Walker, "The Siege of Misrata," Foreign Policy (Jun. 9, 2011), https://foreignpolicy.com/2011/06/09/the-siege-of-misrata-2/.
32. Elif Shafak, "The View From Taksim Square: Why is Turkey Now in Turmoil?," The Guardian (Jun. 3, 2013), https://www.theguardian.com/world/2013/jun/03/taksim-square-istanbul-turkey-protest.

33. "The Running of the Bulls," Bullrun Pamplona, https://www.bullrunpamplona.com/.
34. "Outreach Programme on the 1994 Genocide Against the Tutsi in Rwanda and the United Nations," United Nations, https://www.un.org/en/preventgenocide/rwanda/historical-background.shtml.
35. *See generally,* Lawrence E. Cline, "The Prospects of the Shia Insurgency Movement in Iraq," 20 UNB J. of Conflict Stud. (2000).
36. David Johnston & John M. Broder, "F.B.I. Says Guards Killed 14 Iraqis Without Cause," N.Y. Times (Nov. 14, 2007), https://www.nytimes.com/2007/11/14/world/middleeast/14blackwater.html.
37. Michael A. Newton & Michael P. Scharf, Enemy of the State: The Trial and Execution of Saddam Hussein (St. Martin's Press, Sept. 2008).
38. *Id.* at 71.
39. *Id.* at 74.
40. Public International Law and Policy Group, https://www.publicinternationallawand-policygroup.org/client-update-yemen (last visited Oct. 4, 2021). PILPG hosted Transition Engagement Trainings for geographically diverse civil society organizations engaged in the Yemen peace process in Amman, Jordan.
41. "Ivory Coast Gets Truth and Reconciliation Commission," BBC (Sep. 28, 2011), https://www.bbc.com/news/world-africa-15086829. The Truth and Reconciliation Commission was started by President Alassane Ouattara after a tumultuous post-election period in 2010–2011 in Côte D'Ivoire.
42. "Mitt Romney Lambasted in Attack Ad for Speaking French," BBC (Jan 13, 2012), https://www.bbc.com/news/world-us-canada-16549624.
43. George Santayana, Life of Reason, Reason in Common Sense 284 (Scribner's, 1905) ("Those who cannot remember the past are condemned to repeat it.").
44. *See* Defense Institute of International Legal Studies (DIILS), Defense Security Cooperation Agency, https://www.dsca.mil/defense-institute-international-legal-studies-diils (last visited Oct. 15, 2021).

Contributors

Jacqueline Acho is president of the Acho Group, a leadership coaching and consulting firm, and author of *The Currency of Empathy: The Secret to Thriving in Business and Life*

Madeline Chung is a health disparities researcher from Case Western Reserve University, studying pathophysiology and clinical workflows in the Stanford University-Cleveland Clinic MOST Fellowship and serving as a patient caregiver.

Silvia Fernández de Gurmendi is the 2020 recipient of the Inamori Ethics Prize and a leading figure in international justice, humanitarian law, and human rights and the first woman to serve as president of the International Criminal Court.

Sarah Jordan Reif is an integrated graduate studies student at Case Western Reserve University studying political science, biology, chemistry, and bioethics.

Damon Linder is a PhD student at Tiffin University and is advised by Perry Haan, DBA, professor of marketing in the School of Business.

Lt.Col. Richard A. McConnell, US Army, retired, is an associate professor in the Department of Army Tactics, US Army Command and General Staff College at Fort Leavenworth, Kansas

Khali Mofuoa is a research associate with the Department of Philosophy, University of Pretoria, South Africa.

Michael Scharf is co-dean of the Case Western Reserve University Law School, the Joseph C. Hostetler-BakerHostetler Professor of Law, Director of the Frederick K. Cox International Law Center, and host of *Talking Foreign Policy.*

Lt. Col. Andrew Thueme is an assistant professor in the Department of Army Tactics, US Army Command and General Staff College at Fort Leavenworth, Kansas

Jessica Wolfendale is professor and chair of the Department Philosophy at Marquette University. Her research focuses on the ethics of political violence and the moral psychology of state-sponsored violence.